PULP & PAPER
FLEET

A history of the Quebec and Ontario Transportation Company

D1612125

By Al Sykes and Skip Gillham

ISBN 0-919549-15-2

Printed in Canada

Published by:
Stonehouse Publications
17 Queen Street, St. Catharines, Ontario L2R 5G5
Telephone (416) 684-7251

Cover Photo:
The paper carrier Chicago Tribune spent more years in the Q.&O. fleet
than any other vessel **(Barry Andersen photo)**

Back Cover:
The second Heron Bay — Robert Walton photo
The second Outarde — Basil Nares photo, courtesy Frank Clapp

INTRODUCTION

Many fleets have had a part in developing the Great Lakes and St. Lawrence Seaway transportation network since the dream of William Hamilton Merritt became reality in 1829.

Merritt conceived a plan to by-pass Niagara Falls and thus allow ships to pass between Lake Erie and Lake Ontario. His idea was met with scorn and financial difficulty but he persevered and on November 29, 1829, the schooner Annie and Jane made the first transit of the new waterway.

Three more canals followed and they attracted settlement and growth along the Welland Canal corridor. One of the largest employers was The Ontario Paper Company Limited which built a newsprint mill in Thorold in 1913 and the following year took the first step in developing what became the Quebec and Ontario Transportation Company.

Their goal, as with all successful companies, was efficiency. This meant assembling raw materials at the lowest possible price. As a result a ship, and then ships, were acquired to bring pulpwood to Thorold to produce paper. In time the ships would also be used to deliver the newsprint to the customers.

This was the beginning of "The Pulp and Paper Fleet." Their story as it expanded into a full scale Great Lakes fleet is one of many similar tales of Canadian enterprise and investment. This was a successful story and during the fleet's sixty-nine years on the lakes many other shipping firms were developed only to disappear.

Putting together a history of The Pulp and Paper Fleet and the story of their ships was the idea of Al Sykes. He enlisted the support of Skip Gillham and together they share the responsibility of developing the story into a book.

Without the help of four key people this book would still be only a dream.

Louis Cahill, founder of the public relations firm OEB International and a consultant to the Welland Canals Foundation, was instrumental in getting the authors headed in the right direction.

The right direction was Al Plosz, retired Communications Director for the Ontario Paper Company. He was of immense help in gaining the support of the Company for the project and providing historical date, contacts and photos from the company files.

One of the key contacts was George Corbin. He was a long time Q. & O. employee and former Marine Superintendent for the firm. Mr. Corbin provided photos, checked our facts and made helpful suggestions.

Finally Doug Mackie, Promotion Manager of Stonehouse Publications and the St. Catharines Standard. He developed the cover and oversaw the many details of printing and marketing of The Pulp and Paper Fleet.

We, the authors, are especially grateful to these four men for their assistance, guidance and encouragement. Dreams cannot become reality by themselves.

There were, of course, many others who were of great help. These would certainly include Jim Mitchell. He was formerly part of the Q. & O. family. He provided key information on the cargo runs of the Q. & O. vessels from 1968 to the disbanding of the firm.

Much of the background information on the ships comes from the author's files and these have been accumulated over years of personal research and record keeping.

Many have assisted and we would like to say thank-you to the following whose information has been helpful. These include Barry Andersen, Jay Bascom, John H. Bascom, Dan McCormick, George Ayoub, Rene Beauchamp, Bill Bruce, Ron Graham, Peter Worden, John Vournakis, Emory Massman, Sheldon Straiton, Jim Bartke, Gene Onchulenko, Herbert M. Beazley, Rev. Carl Hall, Bob Campbell, Dick Wicklund, Steve Elve, M.B. Mackay, Jim Roberts, Capt. John Leonard, Capt. Ken Lowes, Capt. Charles Tully, Capt. Frank Cook, Capt. Jim Shires, Capt. Cec Freeman, Chief Engineer Harry Reid and Dave Glick. In addition Alf Sagon-King's work on photo finishing is appreciated.

Others graciously supplied photos. These are acknowledged with the illustrations. Special thanks to Dave Wiley of Great Lakes Graphics in Chicago and Suzette Lopez of the Milwaukee Public Library for their cooperation.

A special thank-you is extended to Lisa Zwarts who did some emergency typing to get the manuscript ready for publishing and did a great job.

We have one more dream. We would like to see more histories of the various shipping enterprises that developed on both sides of the Great Lakes. Ours is not the first such story to be written and we hope others are yet to come.

DEDICATION

This book is dedicated to the thousands of men and women who were part of the Quebec and Ontario Transportation Company over the years and to two women who were not.

The work of the former established Q. & O. as a vital link, not only in the company's transportation network, but also in the Great Lakes and St. Lawrence Seaway scene. The support of the latter, Sue Sykes and Carol Gillham, remains an inspiration to their husbands who wish to say thanks.

WELLAND CANALS FOUNDATION

The Welland Canals Foundation is an outgrowth of the very successful committee established to celebrate the 150th Anniversary of the opening of the Welland Canal.

The Foundation is strictly a volunteer group and operates without any paid staff. They have helped co-ordinate the successful Canal Days programs at various communities along the canal corridor, hosted the annual William Hamilton Merritt Lecture Series in conjunction with Brock University, developed Merritt Day to bring media attention to the Welland Canal as well as being involved in films, T.V. features and news reports on a year around basis.

The encouragement of research and publications about the Welland Canal has been a key focus of Welland Canals Foundation activities and these have resulted in the production of books and postcards. The Pulp and Paper Fleet, written by two members of the Foundation's Board of Directors, is another in the long list of published information developed under Welland Canals Foundation auspices.

ABOUT THE AUTHORS

Al Sykes is a native of Welland, Ontario, and currently resides in the nearby community of Fonthill.

He has had a long interest in the history of the ships of the Great Lakes. From 1976 until 1982 he wrote a series of marine articles for the Welland Evening Tribune. He has also contributed stories to other Ontario newspapers as well as historical journals.

Al works for John Deere in Welland where he is a shipper. His wife Sue and stepsons Rodney and Doug often accompany him on travels around the Great Lakes.

Skip Gillham was born in Toronto and lives in Vineland, Ontario, with his wife Carol and sons Dave and Doug.

He has been writing "Ships That Ply The Lakes" in the St. Catharines Standard since 1970 and a similar series in the Port Huron Times Herald since 1973. He contributes feature articles and news reports to a variety of historical and corporate publications and is the "Niagara News" reporter for "Seaports and the Shipping World." The Pulp and Paper Fleet" is the tenth book he has written or co-authored.

Skip is a Guidance Counsellor, Physical Education teacher and Cross Country Coach at Beamsville District Secondary School in Beamsville, Ontario.

Author's note:

Since we began working on this book the name of The Ontario Paper Company Limited — of which the Q&O was a subsidiary — has been changed. In September 1987, it became the Quebec and Ontario Paper Company Ltd., adopting the name the shipping company had used for many years.

In relating this story, we decided to use the old name to avoid confusion and because the shipping operations were carried out during the time the paper company was known as Ontario Paper Company.

TABLE OF CONTENTS

Col. Robert R. McCormick — on his 74th birthday in 1954 (Q.&O. files)

FOUNDING THE FLEET

The Ontario Transportation and Pulp Company of Thorold was incorporated on January 22, 1914. This wholly owned subsidiary of The Ontario Paper Company began its meager start as a supplier by transporting pulp wood to the Thorold mill from lower Quebec and a deliverer of finished newsprint rolls to the Chicago Tribune warehouse in Chicago.

For the first two and a half years of operation the Ontario Transportation and Pulp Company owned no ships. They relied on the availability of vessels through chartering either by the season or by the trip. This depended on the needs of the Thorold mill and the Chicago Tribune.

Four years prior to the founding of the fleet, Robert R. McCormick, a thirty-year-old lawyer and former politician in the city of Chicago, took an active part in the family newspaper along with his cousin Joseph Medill Patterson. Both men were grandsons of Joseph Medill who had bought an interest in the Tribune 55 years earlier.

They found out that the directors of the newspaper were on the verge of selling the Tribune. McCormick was shocked at the proposal and pursuaded the directors not to sell out and both he and his cousin said they would take an active part in the paper and would turn things around. It didn't take McCormick long to figure out the problems with the paper. Newsprint costs to the Tribune were much higher than those of the rival Hearst papers due to their vast buying power of a larger quantity of newsprint at a cheaper price. A solution had to be found. This seemed to be simple: produce your own newsprint and thus cut your operational costs drastically. Then as the circulation improves, increase the output of your newsprint mill.

Robert McCormick brought his findings to the Board of Directors and he was allowed to spend one million dollars for the building of a paper mill as a subsidiary of the Chicago Tribune. Warren Curtis Jr., a paper mill designer and engineer was contacted by McCormick and with Joseph Medill Patterson looking after the newspaper in Chicago, McCormick was free to venture off with Warren Curtis Jr. in search of a suitable location for the new mill. After inspecting possible sites in Northern Ontario, it was decided to look at towns in Southern Ontario. There the weather was not so harsh and, with towns already developed, the incidental expenditures would be less.

James Battle, a Thorold, Ontario, real estate broker, showed the men the possible sites of the area. These included the final selection of a cow pasture on the banks of the Welland Canal. Battle also acted as an agent for the Ontario Power Company of Niagara Falls and made available to the men enough hydro electric power for the mill project. Other factors that had to be taken into consideration by McCormick and Curtis were the readily available water supply for the mill, the potential use of water transportation as a means of supplying both the mill and the Chicago Tribune, a skilled workforce from the other mills in Thorold, Merritton and St. Catharines and finally the presence of railway lines connecting the Niagara Peninsula with American cities.

The Ontario Paper Company was incorporated on February 29, 1912, with a capital stock of one million dollars held by the Directors of the Tribune Company with the expressed intention to build a newsprint making facility at Thorold, Ontario. Construction orders were given to Warren Curtis Jr. on June 5, 1912, with Curtis in charge of designing and constructing the facility.

The basic idea that Curtis had for the formation of newsprint at the Thorold mill was to have debarked wood pulp brought to the mill. There, electric grinders would reduce the wood to pulp to be fed to the steam turbine driven newsprint machines.

The revolutionary ideas put forth by Curtis had many skeptics. But the first machine was put into production on September 5, 1913, and the second machine started up on November 14. The output of both machines was far less than had been expected. However, after the fine tuning, the machine's production gradually increased satisfying both Robert R. McCormick, President of the Tribune company and Warren Curtis Jr., who had been appointed President and General Manager of the Thorold mill. The latter held this position from 1913 until his death in 1930.

As the paper mill was being erected, docks and storage areas for the newsprint and wood pulp were being constructed on the banks of the Welland Canal. The depth of the water at the dock had to be dredged to the maximum canal draft and concrete facings built for the docks. Whirly cranes were placed on the docks to load and unload the ships of wood pulp and paper plus coal. The latter would be used in the boiler house.

Another problem facing Robert McCormick was the availability of timber rights in Ontario to supply his mill. He was turned down by the Ministry of Crown Lands of Ontario in an attempt to secure timber in that province. This forced him to purchase pulpwood on the open market in Toronto from timber agents. Although this temporarily relieved the problem of a source of raw materials, it only put off the actual leasing of land and timber rights.

With the Thorold mill in production, it now became apparent that water transportation would be the cheapest and easiest way to ship the products used by and produced at Thorold. Rail transportation had been used to get the mill running but this was not satisfactory to Robert McCormick. He then formed the Ontario Transportation and Pulp Company on January 22, 1914, and had the newly built steamer Honereva of the Donald Steamship of England chartered. The deal included an option in the contract for an outright purchase if desired.

The Honereva was of canal size dimensions and could haul 850 cords of pulpwood per trip. It was used to haul wood pulp from Anticosti Island on the St. Lawrence River to Thorold. Once light, the ship would sail to Sodus Point, N.Y., or Rochester, N.Y., on Lake Ontario and load coal for Montreal or other ports along the St. Lawrence River. This move had the ship making money for the new company.

The task of shipping the newsprint westward was handled by the Rutland Transit Company, a subsidiary of the Rutland Railroad. It extended rail service from New York City to Montreal by connecting with the Canadian National Railway. The Rutland Transit Company operated its own fleet of steamers from Ogdensburg, New York, to Chicago, Illinois. This route ran right past the front door of the Thorold mill. The steamers did not have to go out of their way to service the Ontario Paper Company. They learned that newsprint stored in the hull of the ships remained dry throughout the four day voyage proving water transportation to be an economical success.

Joseph Medill Patterson (Q.&O. files)

On December 4, 1915, the Ontario Paper Company purchased 312 square miles of timber lands at the mouth of the Rocky River, twenty-five miles west of Seven Islands, Quebec. This remote area of the lower St. Lawrence River was renamed Shelter Bay by Robert McCormick and is known today as Port Cartier. Soon the United States was involved in the hostilities and Robert McCormick was a reserve Colonel. This prevented any further progress at Shelter Bay. So it was not until 1919 that the north shore would be developed by McCormick.

Before being called to active military service, Robert McCormick purchased the steamer Honereva on August 17, 1916. This ship had the distinction of being the first vessel in "The Pulp and Paper Fleet." However, her ownership would last but one full week. Honereva had been spotted by French Maritime owners. They desperately needed tonnage to haul supplies to Europe. She was sold on August 24 to the French Government and soon renamed.

The profits from the sale of the Honereva were enough to purchase the company's second ship. Toiler was acquired from James Playfair of Midland at a price of $90,706. The Toiler had recently been converted to steam power. This replaced a diesel power plant which had been originally placed in the ship by her builders in 1911.

Toiler's hold could take up to 1000 cords of wood and this made her that much more of an asset to the company. The living conditions on the Toiler were less comfortable and McCormick had all cabins refurbished with the addition of shower baths. This was considered a real luxury and thus he set the standard that would be followed on ships of the fleet for years to come.

Two further purchases by the Ontario Transportation and Pulp Company took place in 1916. The steamer Mary H. Boyce and the schooner barge Middlesex were to augment the expanded needs put upon the steamship company by the increased outputs of the Ontario Paper Company. The Boyce was used to tow the barge between the St. Lawrence and Thorold. The Boyce, with a capacity of 430 cords of wood or 800 tons of coal, and the Middlesex, with a capacity of 1100 tons of coal, were definite assets. They helped relieve the tonnage requirements placed on the Toiler which by now was also active in the Chicago newsprint run.

Both Joseph Medill Patterson and Robert R. McCormick were in active service in 1917 and sent overseas. In their absence William H. Field was appointed general manager in charge of all the Chicago Tribune enterprises. These included the steamship company. Captain Henry Louis St. James de Beauvais was hired at this time as the company's first Marine Superintendent. He was responsible for ship maintenance.

Also hired in 1917 was Elbert M. Antrim as Tribune Company's Traffic Manager. His duties were the arrangement of cargoes, warehousing, insurance for the ships and cargo and other related items. His first big problem came on August 13, 1917, when the Middlesex stranded near Morrisburg, Ontario, in the St. Lawrence River. The tow line parted during a storm and the barge wrecked. She was sold to the insurance underwriters who eventually salvaged the schooner barge and had her rebuilt.

Warren Curtis Jr. designed the Thorold Mill (Q.&O. files)

Linden was an early member of the fleet (Q.&O. files)

THE EARLY YEARS

With the war raging on in Europe, both McCormick and Patterson served in the battlefields of France. Their interests in the United States and Canada prospered as the Tribune grew in circulation and the paper mill in Thorold was able to meet the demand. The steamers Toiler and Mary H. Boyce were busy filling cargo commitments.

The effect of the war on the cost of ship tonnage became more apparent in the spring of 1918. General Manager Field was offered and accepted a bid for the canal steamer Toiler for the sum of $350,000. This move drastically cut the trip capacity of the fleet and although the Toiler fetched a handsome profit for the company finding a suitable replacement was another problem.

Finally, after scouring the lakes, the steamer Linden was purchased and brought into Canadian registry. Because her capacity of 571 cords of wood was a little less than half that of Toiler, more chartering of steamers was needed to meet peak demands.

The Linden, an 1895 product of Jenks Shipbuilding of Port Huron, was wooden hulled and smaller than the maximum dimensions allowed through the St. Lawrence canals. Another drawback was her lack of a salt water condenser. One was found in Georgia and shipped to Buffalo for installation in the steamer.

With the armistice, both Patterson and McCormick were discharged, and returned to Chicago to take over the Tribune organization once again. Increased outputs of newsprint at Thorold due to the installation of two more paper machines in 1917 and 1919 helped to keep up with the increasing demands by the Chicago Tribune. Circulation had grown as their rival papers decreased.

McCormick and Patterson decided to begin a second newspaper in New York City. The tabloid style Illustrated Daily News started off slowly in 1919 but gradually rose in circulation to over 200,000 copies per day. The added burden for more newsprint was placed on the Thorold mill and, in turn, brought about the development of the timber limits at Shelter Bay, Quebec , in 1919.

Arthur A. Schmon, a former captain who served under McCormick in France, was given the job of building and managing the pulpwood operations at Shelter Bay. The town had to be built with homes for the staff and wood cutters. Also constructed were dams, logging booms and a dock for the loading of the pulpwood. All supplies had to arrive by ship before the freeze up which left the inhabitants isolated until the following spring.

Arthur Schmon was left with a very large responsibility. With the co-operation of the workmen the town of Shelter Bay rose and grew to its present day inhabitation under the name Port Cartier. The company steamers often unloaded their cargoes of coal at Montreal where they would reload supplies for the town. Everything had to be shipped into Shelter Bay by water and the company owned vessels played a major role in forming the town.

Arthur A. Schmon developed Shelter Bay (Q.&O. files)

Actual shipping of the pulpwood westward to the Thorold mill began in the spring of 1923. Woodsmen had spent the previous winter cutting the logs and storing them in the Rocky River. Spring thaw allowed them to be driven down river to the flumes at Shelter Bay and loaded on the new dock into the steamer's hold.

The increased pulpwood demand of the Thorold mill was placed on the two steamers Boyce and Linden. Additional chartering became an expensive endeavour and forced the company to order its first two new steamers in early 1922. The British shipyard of Swan, Hunter and Wigham Richardson Ltd. received the contract to build Hull 1187 which was named the Chicago Tribune. The North of Ireland Shipbuilding Company Ltd. of Londonderry was awarded the contract for the second steel canaller. Their Hull 101 was named New York News. Both ships were named after the newspapers which were owned by the Tribune company. The ships had a capacity of 1,100 cords of pulpwood or approximately 2,300 tons at the maximum canal draft of 14 feet.

One new feature to the steamers was the large C and small T located on the stack of the ship honouring the Chicago Tribune organization. Although the Ontario Transportation and Pulp Company remained the official name of the company until 1933, ships were often listed as being owned by the Chicago Tribune Transportation Company.

Both steamers successfully passed their trials in England and loaded Welsh coal for Montreal. They arrived safely in Canada in the summer of 1922. These new acquisitions meant that the Linden and Mary H. Boyce were now expendable. The Boyce was sold to N.M. Paterson of Fort William in 1922 while the Linden was sold in 1923 to Mr. R. Burns of Detroit.

More timber limits were purchased at Franquelin in 1920 and further acquisitions in 1921 by Ontario Paper Company gave the company an expansion of over 262 square miles of woodlands. This tied in with a further development at the Thorold mill. A fifth paper machine was added to give the company an output in 1921 of 81,140 tons of newsprint to feed the growing demand of the newspapers.

Engineers were sent to the Quebec North Shore in 1922 with the intention of developing a pulp mill and using the Outardes River as a source of hydro-electric power. Construction on the power dam commenced during the winter of 1925-26.

The Ontario Transportation and Pulp Company opened offices in Montreal on McGill Street in 1922 as a means of closer contact between the developing settlements in lower Quebec and the Thorold paper mill. In 1923, the first full season of operation for the two new canallers, the Chicago Tribune was under the command of Captain R. J. Wilson with L. Vipond serving as her Chief Engineer. On the New York News, Captain J. V. Norris was in command with Emery Scott in charge of the engine room. All four men were competent navigators and engineers upholding the standards demanded by the owners.

Winter quarters for the two ships would normally be at Thorold where ship maintenance would be performed which did not necessitate drydocking. Hull plate repair was usually carried out at Montreal or Lauzon, Quebec.

Further expansion and modernization of the Thorold mill commenced in the summer of 1927. This coupled with the increased demands for newsprint by the papers in Chicago and New York put a further strain on handling that commodity to both cities. Rail costs to New York and Chicago increased and the railways did not think that the Tribune Company would balk at the increase. To their surprise a contract was let in the fall of 1929 to Earles Ship-

building and Engineering Limited for a canal size vessel. This diesel powered ship was to be the first designed specifically to transport newsprint from Thorold to Chicago. A raised trunk deck allowed the stowage of several hundred extra rolls of newsprint. This cut the operational costs of the ship since it would run on the upper lakes where she would not be restricted by low water drafts dictated by the lower St. Lawrence River canals.

The name Thorold was chosen and, after her trials in late May of 1930, she sailed to Canada with a cargo of China clay from Finley, England. She then began regular duty clearing Thorold with newsprint for Chicago and returning in ballast.

This trade continued regularly for the next decade. In 1933, for example, the Thorold made a total of 18 round trips beginning on April 23 upbound with paper and arriving back at Thorold for winter quarters on December 4. One novel feature for the Thorold was a tennis court painted in the hold. This could be used by the crew as a form of exercise between their 6 hour watches. Billboard sized advertising was put on the hull which read "3,000 tons of paper for the Chicago Tribune."

A further purchase in 1933 of the canaller Belvoir was required to check further rail increases to New York City. Belvoir would load newsprint at Thorold and sail down the St. Lawrence River along the east coast to New York City to discharge. This was cheaper than the existing rail route. She then sailed to Reading, New Jersey, where she would take on coal for a St. Lawrence River port. This route continued for two seasons until the railways were forced to cut their rates and free the ship for use on the lakes.

The Ontario Paper Company plant developed along the Welland Canal at Thorold, Ontario (Q.&O. files)

EXPANSION AND THE WAR

A reorganization of the company took place in 1932. The Ontario Transportation and Pulp Company Limited was renamed the Quebec and Ontario Transportation Company Limited of Montreal. A complete name change for ships in the fleet was announced in December of 1933 as all four lay at their winter berths at the Thorold paper dock.

The diesel canaller Thorold was renamed Chicago Tribune as it was felt that the newest ship, which was designed purposely to serve the needs of the Chicago Tribune, should be named after the newspaper. The original Chicago Tribune was renamed Thorold in recognition of the town which was the home of Ontario Paper Company. The New York News became Shelter Bay in honour of the loading port for pulpwood destined for the Thorold paper mill. Finally, the newly acquired Belvoir was renamed New York News as the ship had been bought to deliver newsprint there.

The appointments for 1933 included Capt. R.S. Brown and Chief Engineer H. Collins for Thorold, Capt. F.V. McIntyre and Chief J.F. Duncan of New York New and Capt. George Ferguson and Chief L. Vipond for Chicago Tribune.

As the Depression continued through the 1930's the four-ship fleet kept active throughout the entire season. This gave the crews, which averaged 19 men per ship, stability through the tough times when jobs were scarce. Unemployed men would line the canal lock walls asking each captain for a job. Berths on the Q.&O. ships were quickly filled and the sailors would stay with the vessel knowing quite well that their chances of getting on with another company ship were nil if they decided to leave part way through the year.

BELVOIR was purchased to deliver newsprint to New York. (Ken Lowes collection)

CHICAGO TRIBUNE (L) and THOROLD frequently wintered at the company dock at Thorold (Ken Lowes Collection)

In September 1935, the vessels of the Q.&O. fleet engaged in an unusual regatta for the Colonel R.R. McCormick Trophy.

Each steamer was to provide a crew for a lifeboat rowing race over a measured half mile course of the Welland Canal between the sulphur dock at Thorold to just above the N.S.&T. Railroad bridge. As all vessels were not at Thorold at one time, they had to race against the clock.

Each crew rowed down the course, took an eight minute break, and rowed back. The total time taken established the winning team. The men from the Thorold covered the mile in nine minutes, four and a half seconds and were declared champions.

Despite a 40% increase of production in the 1930s, the Thorold mill was unable to meet the increasing demands for newsprint at both Chicago and New York City. It became apparent that another paper mill should be built in the province of Quebec. Arthur Schmon had succeeded the late Warren Curtis Jr. as head of operations in Ontario and Quebec, and his studies indicated that building a paper mill on the North Shore would be cheaper than expanding at Thorold or building at Quebec City. In 1936, after considerable deliberation, contruction of a paper mill at Baie Comeau was started along with the building of the town of Baie Comeau.

The crew of New York News with Capt. Brown took second.
They were the heaviest team with an average weight of 172 lbs. (Q.&O. files)

The 1935 Regatta officials were J.B. Sims judge, W.S. Coolin starter, and J.M. Deeney timer (Q.&O. files)

**Fred Byington Jr. was in charge of building
Baie Comeau (Q.&O. files)**

Without ships, the Baie Comeau project could not have been undertaken. There was no railroad to the area, and no highway. Everything had to be brought in by ships operated, or chartered by the Q.&O. In 1937 alone more than 140,000 tons of materials and supplies — everything from generators to buttons — had to be brought in to the Baie Comeau dock; enough to fill a freight train 43 miles long.

Meanwhile as this expansion of the North Shore was being planned it became evident that still more tonnage would be needed to supply the demands of the new mill plus offset chartered tonnage that was still being used at peak times in the transporting of pulpwood to Thorold. Through the efforts of the engineering department at Ontario Paper and the naval architects Lambert & German of Montreal an all welded ship was designed. The British yard of Swan, Hunter & Wigham Richardson of Wallsend-on-Tyne, England was awarded the contract to build this new, innovative canaller. It would be the largest vessel of this type to transit the lower canals and would have the capability of carrying greater cargoes than any previous canaller. After a successsful launch on July 4, 1935, the Joseph Medill was readied for her transatlantic crossing. She completed her sea trials on the 10th of August and cleared Leith, Scotland, with a cargo of coal for Montreal. The ship was sighted by a Norwegian passenger ship on the 17th but never seen again. All crewmen went down with the ship.

Undaunted by this tragic loss, Quebec and Ontario officials still felt the design of the Joseph Medill was practical and they ordered another canaller of similar proportions in 1936. Superstitious of the past results, the company decided to name this new canaller the Franquelin in honour of the pulpwood loading port on the North Shore of the St. Lawrence. Franquelin had a better trip across the Atlantic and arrived safely at Montreal on May 29, 1936, bringing a cargo of China clay. This fifth ship for the fleet of pulp and paper carriers was designed for maximum stowage of cargo in her hull in the restricted depths of the lower canals. Her capacity of 1360 cords set tonnage records for the lower canals. A former master noted that she had a clearance of barely a foot to enter

the lower locks and the gates of the lock embraced her stern as she was snuggled up into the lock.

Franquelin would load coal or grain for her downbound trip, often with record breaking results in both commodities. Once unloaded at Montreal, she would reload supplies for the construction at Baie Comeau. It was common for the ship to take bags of cement with deck loads of steel or machinery for the paper mill. One rather unusual cargo sent down the St. Lawrence had the Franquelin loading two cargo holds of beer, augmented with other supplies in the remaining two holds.

The late 1930's marked increased expansion of all the Chicago Tribune subsidiaries. The Ontario Paper Company leased timber limits at Heron Bay, Ontario, in the spring of 1937 and commenced to set up lumber camps and construct a loading dock for ships on the shores of Lake Superior. On December 23, 1937, the first of two paper machines was started up at Baie Comeau. The second came into production one month later. This brought about the chartering of deep sea ships to transport the newsprint produced at Baie Comeau to New York City. A subsidiary company, the Illinois Atlantic Company, was formed to handle this traffic. They purchased the Colabee in May, 1940.

With the expansion into Ontario timber limits two more ships were added to the fleet in 1939. The canaller Brulin, with a capacity of 1295 cords of wood or 2050 tons of paper, was purchased to supply Thorold with pulpwood from St. Lawrence ports. She was renamed Outarde. Also added was the 389 foot upper laker Robert P. Durham. She was renamed Heron Bay and had a carrying capacity of 5,500 tons.

The closing of the 1939 season found Quebec and Ontario Transportation in the position of owning one upper laker and six canallers. With the Second World War erupting in Europe the previous September the coming shipping season would bring about changes with the fleets of the Great Lakes.

The previous use of canallers in Britain during the First World War had not been forgotten by the British War Ministry. Their accessibility to small ports along the coast freed up larger ships to move supplies to Europe from North America. Therefore, it was no surprise to the Canadian vessel owners when, in June 1940, the British government requisitioned a group of canallers for service around England. Among this first group of ships to leave the lakes was the Quebec and Ontario canaller Thorold. She cleared Canada in late June with a British crew and a cargo of saw logs. Her crossing was successful but on the first trip along the Bristish coast Thorold was attacked and sunk by German aircraft. Eleven men, including her captain, were lost.

Further problems arose as the war increased to involve the United States. The Colabee was requisitioned by the United States Maritime Commission for use in supplying the American war effort. This eliminated ocean steamers for delivering newsprint to New York City from Baie Comeau. An alternate route to deliver the newsprint had to be found so it was decided to ship the newsprint from Baie Comeau up the St. Lawrence River to Oswego, New York. There the cargo could be transshipped into barges

FRANQUELIN loading pulpwood at Baie Comeau (courtesy Lou Cahill)

The stack of the first OUTARDE reveals the company colours (Ken Lowes Collection)

or chartered motor ships of the Federal Motorship Corporation for the trip through the New York Barge Canal to New York City. Once these barges and motor ships were discharged in New York they would load cargoes of bauxite which is used in the production of aluminum in the smelters of Port Alfred, Quebec. Although difficult at times, service to New York was continued throughout the war and the New York Daily received a regular supply of newsprint.

One light hearted letter addressed to L. McMillan, then Superintendent of Engineering in 1940, from Captain William Redfern, master of the canaller Outarde on the problem of drying a hold of grain dust helped to relieve the apparent tensions of sailing during these times. He replied, "While you offer several good suggestions, which might work out to the advantage of the ship, I wonder about using a water hose. It will take some time to dry this hold to be ready for grain, or should I say paper. As for the dust, that is neither here nor there.

He went on to say, "If any of these ideas that you suggest do not work out to the advantage of the ship, I would like to propose this idea. Buy at least thirty hens, Plymouth Rocks. As the Outarde has three holds, put ten chickens down each hold after unloading grain. They will clean it up, and the feed does not cost anything. In return we get eggs, which we are paying today's market price of 43¢ a dozen. Now there is an idea to think over. I'll be glad to talk the situation over with you on my return to Thorold. Yours truly, W. E. Redfern."

The trips eastward from Montreal were done with absolute radio silence as not to tip off roving U-Boat captains of traffic movements. There were many anxious hours of waiting at both Montreal, Baie Comeau and Franquelin

The hold of COLABEE carried rolls of newsprint (Q.&O. files)

as the canallers plodded along to their destinations. Only on arrival were telegraphed messages sent in code alerting management of the safe arrival of the ships at their destinations. They then received orders for their return voyage.

In 1942 the Canadian Government requisitioned the canallers New York News and Outarde from the Q.&O. fleet. Both canallers were given the war grey colours in an effort to blend in with the ocean, and they were dispatched to the Gulf of St. Lawrence to transport goods along the east cost. During the winter months the ships were used to haul coal from Norfolk, Virginia, to Boston. Both ships returned to Q.&O. in 1943. The New York

News was handed back on May 9 while the Outarde returned to Q.&O. control on June 13. Outarde had suffered a grounding near St. Pierre and Miquelon Islands during her war runs and was repaired at Norfolk, Virginia. The New York News suffered no major incidents during this era.

With the armistice in 1945, Quebec and Ontario Transportation was ready to enter the post war era with a fleet of six ships consisting of 5 canallers and the upper laker Heron Bay. Meanwhile the Illinois Atlantic Corporation received the Colabee from the United States Maritime Commission and she was put back into her regular run from Baie Comeau to New York City.

RICHARD J. BARNES was one of the ships chartered to carry newsprint to New York during the war (Q.&O. files)

POST-WAR GROWTH

The post war years brought The Quebec and Ontario Transportation Company face to face with two serious labor disputes. A strike by cutters at Heron Bay in 1946 virtually closed the loading operations for several months until the dispute could be settled.

A walk-out by the Canadian Seamen's Union in May 1946 shut down most lake operators. The Quebec and Ontario Transportation Company was an exception as they had a contract with the union. So wood and paper continued to flow to and from Thorold and Baie Comeau while ships chartered by the company were tied to the wall until the end of the dispute. Officials from Q.&O. helped bring the shipowners and unions representatives together to iron out the difficulties and end the strike. There were further labour problems until 1950 when company sailors chose to join the Seafarers' International Union.

Further expansion of Ontario timber limits at Manitoulin Island in 1947 put new burdens on the Q.&O. fleet. A total of 78,000 acres of Manitoulin and Cockburn Island woodlands consisting of poplar, spruce and balsam were at the company's disposal. Woodcutting commenced during the 1947-48 winter and since there were no suitable docks available at this area it was decided to use a floating jack ladder to load the ships with wood from log booms.

As the 1948 season commenced the fleet was in the charge of General Manager Earl Collison who had been with the company since 1937, A.G. Sweeting was the Superintendent of Engineering and the company fleet consisted of the following ships: Chicago Tribune, F.V. McIntyre Master, M. McLeod Chief Engineer, Franquelin, J. O. Beaudoin Master, R. Peatman Chief, Heron Bay, G. Ferguson Master, A. Steward Chief, New York News,

The Officer's Meeting of 1948 included the following: Front, L-R. Capt. Redfern, Capt. Dave Gendron, Capt. Fred McIntyre, Back: Capt. Ferguson, Capt. Brown and Capt. Beaudin (Q.&O. files)

FRANQUELIN brought a deckload of groundwood pulp from Baie Comeau to Thorold on her first trip of 1948.
(Editorial Associates photo — Q.&O. files)

14

R. J. Brown Master, G. Coffin Chief, Outarde, W. E. Redfern Master, W. Martin Chief, and Shelter Bay, D. Gendron Master, W. Smith Chief.

A further addition to the fleet in 1948 was the acquisition of the canaller Empire Rother from the British Ministry of War Transport. This vessel formerly operated on the lakes prior to the Second World War under the name Delaware of St. Lawrence Steamships Limited. After a full refit in England, the canaller sailed to Canada under her new name of Manicouagan.

In 1946 limits along the Black River section of Heron Bay consisting of 100 square miles of timberlands were leased from the Ontario government through the negotiations of Arthur Schmon. Two years later further negotiations resulted in the acquisition of the assets of Eddie Johnson (Pineland Timber Company). These included 546 square miles of Crown lands plus all developments made by the former owner including roads, dams, lumber camps plus a diesel electric powered tug Satin Leaf and two steel consort barges named Merle H. and Blanche H. This purchase tied in perfectly with the Heron Bay operations as the flume at Heron Bay could be used to load pulpwood cut on these limits. The acquisition of the two barges renamed Pic River and Black River, also helped ease the problem of excess tonnage required to handle the pulp needs of the Thorold mill. The tug, now the Rocky River,

would tow the barges from Thorold to Chicago with newsprint and then, after unloading, they would be shuttled to South Chicago where they would load coal cargoes destined for Midland, Little Current or Britt on Georgian Bay. After unloading they would take on pulpwood at either Heron Bay or Gore Bay for Thorold. The barges were almost constantly carrying cargo. This helped offset the costs of the diesel electric tug but it meant a slower speed and shortened operating season due to insurance and maritime regulations.

In 1951, while in their third year of operation with the company, it was decided to refit both the Pic River and Black River at Port Weller Dry Docks with diesel engines. Under the direction of Marine Superintendent Bill Roos, the job of cutting off the sterns of the barges and installing diesels plus adding cabins fore and aft quickly took shape. Black River was completed in the fall of 1952 and Pic River during the following winter. Both vessels were very successful.

Adding diesels to the tow barges made the tug Rocky River excess tonnage to the needs of Q.&O. She was sold in 1953 to the Foundation Maritime Company of Halifax.

The early 1950's saw demands for a new and larger seaway. Parliament wanted to make the Great Lakes readily accessible to larger deep sea salties and to allow upper lakers to travel eastward with grain cargoes to elevators

Jack ladders were used to load vessels such as BLACK RIVER at Manitoulin Island
(Editorial Associates — Q.&O. files)

Vessels loaded at the dock at Franquelin (Q.&O. files)

WASHINGTON TIMES HERALD joins R.H. Marshall loading at Shelter Bay in September 1952
(Editorial Associates — Q.&O. files)

along the St. Lawrence River. Newly discovered iron ore ranges in Northern Quebec increased demands and soon the project of building a St. Lawrence Seaway proceeded through the co-operation of the Canadian and United States governments.

A further addition to the fleet of Q.&O. was required to meet increased pulp and paper demands from lower Quebec during the 1954 season. This brought about the building of two all welded twin screw canallers by Atlantic Shipbuilding Company of Newport, Wales. Both ships had minimal power and were constructed in such a manner as to prohibit their lengthening with the addition of a new midbody several years later. This was not the case with most of the canallers built in the 1950's.

The first of the ships to come to Canada was the motor vessel Baie Comeau. She arrived at Montreal on October 18, 1954. The second ship, the motor vessel Manicouagan, arrived in Montreal the following year on July 1, 1955. Both ships were renamed later that season to Joseph Medill Patterson and Col. Robert R. McCormick in honour of the two men who had brought about the founding of the fleet forty-one years earlier.

Changes were also taking place with the Illinois Atlantic Company. On June 28, 1950, the Colabee was sold to American interests and was replaced by the chartered Norwegian salty Elin Hope. It was found that the chartering of foreign tonnage was more economical than operating the Colabee. The Elin Hope would continue for the next decade carrying newsprint at an average trip capacity of 5,800 tons of newsprint from Baie Comeau to New York City.

With the closing of the 1958 season the Quebec and Ontario Transportation looked ahead to many changes associated with the opening the following year of the St. Lawrence Seaway. Changes in the size and number of ships was just around the corner as was a new twist in the shipping business, tolls on the Seaway and the Welland Canal. As the 1958 season ended the Q.&O. fleet numbered 10 vessels consisting of 7 canal size ships and 3 upper lakers.

The next change to come in the fleet was the sale in 1958 of the canaller Shelter Bay to N.M. Patterson of Fort William. The Shelter Bay was the oldest member of the fleet of canallers and, as New York News was the first ship to be built for the company. Her sister, the Thorold, was lost in 1940. They had served their owners well and both ships were the backbone of the fleet in its early years.

L-R. COL. ROBERT R. McCORMICK, CHICAGO TRIBUNE, FRANQUELIN and BLACK RIVER are idle at Thorold for the winter (Q.&O. files)

George Coffin at the main engine of THOROLD (Sam Preval Studio — Q.&O. files)

THE SHIPS AND THE SEAWAY

A great influx of salt water traffic came to the lakes in 1959. There was still uncertainty among vessel owners as to how this influx would affect commodities to be hauled through the system. Quebec and Ontario Transportation began to diversify to other bulk commodities to turn the shipping season into a more profitable one. More grain and iron ore cargoes were obtained to keep the ships regularly loaded and help to offset the newly installed tolls on the canals.

However, it soon became apparent that changes in the fleet would have to come. Other operators quickly sold off their smaller canallers for scrap in 1959. Q.&O. disposed of Outarde in 1960 to Buckport Shipping of Montreal. Next to become surplus to the needs of Q.&O. was the New York News. She was also sold to Buckport Shipping in 1962. Then, the Heron Bay was sold to Federal Commerce and Navigation Company of Montreal. The final ship to pass out of the fleet in 1962 was the canaller Manitoulin. She was sold to A. Newman & Co. of St. Catharines for scrap.

To offset these sales, Q.&O. increased tonnage in the fleet through a newly created subsidiary called Comet Enterprises of Hamilton, Bermuda. They purchased the Michael K. Tewksbury and Carmi A. Thompson and both ships were towed from Buffalo to Port Colborne in December 1962 for a preliminary refit prior to entering their new trades the following spring. Another change was the addition of a sixty foot section to the midbody of the Chicago Tribune. This, along with a prior re-engining of the ship, ensured her economical future for years to come.

The new upper lakers became Outarde and Thorold and they could carry larger quantities of pulpwood. They also hauled paper to Chicago and on occasion would venture down the Seaway with grain and return up the lakes with iron ore for Lake Erie or Michigan ports.

In 1960 the charter on the Elin Hope was dropped in favor of the motor vessel Baie Comeau. Both ships operated year round in this service but the Baie Comeau with oversize high speed cargo gear was newer and more suited for the severe winter conditions of the St. Lawrence.

In 1965 another change occurred with the purchase of the upper laker Jay C. Morse. She was renamed Shelter Bay. Also 1965 marked the final season of water shipments of pulpwood from Heron Bay. All further pulp cargoes to the Thorold mill from their Ontario limits, would come by rail. The company began to diversify and actively pursue other cargoes.

Also in 1965 the movement of newsprint from Baie Comeau to Chicago rose dramatically thus justifying additional tonnage being purchased. At the end of the season Comet Enterprises purchased the upper laker J. Pierpont Morgan from United States Steel. This ship was towed to the Port Arthur shipyard for survey in December of 1965 and she was ready for service the following spring. This made the company a nine ship fleet.

W. Earl Collison served the company for many years (Q.&O. files)

Office personnel changes had taken place during the fifties and sixties. George Corbin replaced Bill Roos as Marine Superintendent in September 1956 while Earl Collison remained as Vice President and General Manager. Robert W. Savage joined the company as Assistant Manager in 1965.

In 1967 Q.&O. purchased the stretched canallers Griffon and Tecumseh from the Mohawk Navigation Company of Montreal. Both ships had been built in the mid 1950's at Port Weller Drydocks and were proven carriers. They replaced the canaller Franquelin, which had been sold off in 1964, plus the Col. Robert R. McCormick and Joseph Medill Patterson. The latter pair were decommissioned part way into the 1967 season. Eventually all three former Q.&O. canallers saw further service in the Caribbean trades. The two new additions to the fleet had limited coastal classification which broadened their trading capabilities.

The 1969 shipping season marked the 55th year of operation for the Q.&O. fleet. That year appointments for the nine ship fleet were as follows; Heron Bay: Cecil Freeman Master, Barney Adam Chief, Shelter Bay: Walter Carpenter Master, Murdo Smith Chief, Thorold: Dave Gendron Master, E. Cascanette Chief, Outarde: Eric Penney Master, Stanley Smith Chief, Franquelin: Wm. Thoms Master, William McCaffery Chief, New York News: Ivan Caron Master, Paul Peloquin Chief, Chicago Tribune: James Shires Master, Edgar Harris Chief, Pic River: James Ferguson Master, Raymond Peatman Chief, Black River: Fred Bingham Master, Alvin Williams Chief. For that season a total of 236 cargoes were handled by the nine ships with grain making up one third of the total. Salt was the second largest commodity hauled followed by newsprint, pulpwood, iron ore and coal. Other shipments hauled with less frequency that season were; coke, clay, pig iron, sugar, steel, pitch, groundwood and gravel. It was obvious that the diversification of the fleet into other bulk trades was having a sound effect on the company. The augmenting of other bulk cargoes with the grain helped keep the ships active for the entire season. A grain crop failure put many other carriers to the wall or in other cases to the scrapyard but with these other contracts in hand Q.&O. management turned what could have been a dismal season into a profitable one.

A grounding accident involving the steamer Thorold in 1971 forced the retirement of the ship in December of that season and she was sold to Marine Salvage of Port Colborne. Thorold was renamed Thoro at the Rameys Bend yard to free the name for the company's next purchase, the salt water ship Gosforth.

The Gosforth, built in 1962, was purchased July 1, 1972, by Trico Enterprises Limited of Hamilton, Bermuda, and chartered to Q.&O.. Her first trip was in late July when she cleared Baie Comeau with newsprint for Florida.

A further addition to the fleet took place in January of 1973 with the purchase of the steam turbine driven ship Golden Hind by Trico. The Golden Hind, with a capacity of 16,000 tons, was the largest carrier in the fleet and showed that the company was making an effort to expand their trip capacity as they modernized. The fleet was reduced by one ship at the end of the season when the Outarde was laid up in Montreal and sold for scrap.

In an effort to streamline company business and at the same time cut costs, the offices at Montreal were closed in 1972 and moved to St. Catharines. With the company venturing into different bulk trades it was more ad-

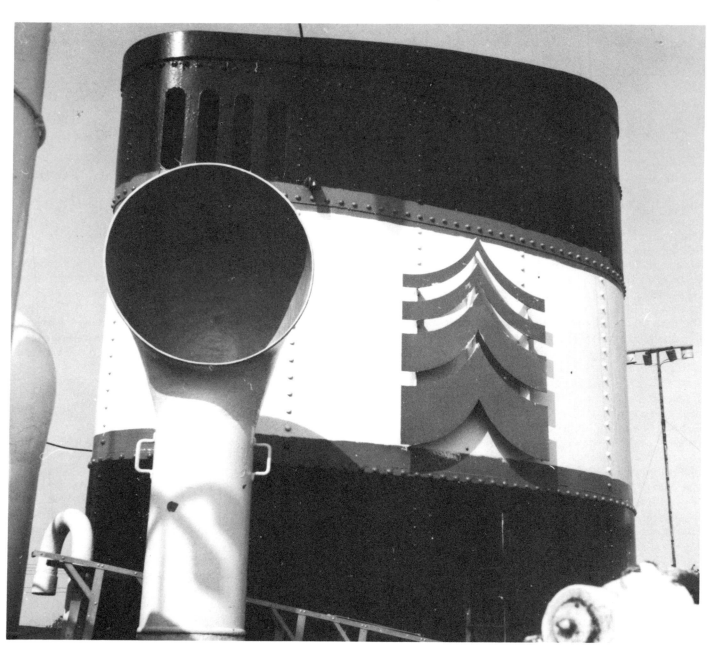

The new stack design is shown on PIC RIVER on September 17, 1972 (SG)

HELEN EVANS stopped at Halifax on September 23, 1980, enroute to scrapping in South America
(M.B. Mackay photo)

vantageous to be located by the Welland Canal.

Shipments of newsprint from Thorold in Q.&O. ships ceased in 1972 as a cut in rail rates made it more economical to use the railroad to supply paper to Chicago. Also at this time it was announced that 1973 would be the last year in which pulpwood would be shipped from Baie Comeau to Thorold on lake vessels. These two mainstays of the past for the company now permanently changed the character of their activities. No longer would the Pulp and Paper Fleet be recognized by its deckloads of pulp or tarpaulins covering tons of newsprint.

A further change was the designing of a new house flag and stack emblem for the fleet. Gone was the familiar red and yellow funnel with white Q.&O. initials. In its place was a blue, white and black stack with a blue logo in the middle representing waves.

In September of 1975, Q.&O. purchased the steamer Robert Hobson from Marine Salvage. The Hobson, of 1926 vintage, was renamed the Outarde. She was a coal burning ship and had to be converted over to oil the following winter as there were no coal bunkering facilities east of Port Colborne. She had been operated previously in the American ore trades and although uneconomical on this run she was an excellent addition to the fleet.

Baie Comeau II, a salty formerly named Monte Almanzor, was purchased by Q.&O. in 1977 and refitted at Port Colborne. This ship was used primarily to aid the hauling of newsprint out of Baie Comeau south to markets along the eastern seaboard.

In 1978 a major purchase by the company saw the fleet enlarge by five vessels. The Hindman Tranportation Company of Owen Sound was acquired after negotiations between Robert Savage, now president of the Q.&O. and Howard Hindman. This brought the fleet up to sixteen ships and was the most to ever sail under this company's direction. Of this group of five, the George Hindman and Blanche Hindman were purchased at full market value while the three older ships, Martha Hindman, Helen Evans and Parker Evans were taken at scrap value. It became apparent that the three latter ships would not be in Q.&O. colors for long as their age and size did not make them very economical to operate. The fall of 1978 brought about the first major reduction of this fleet. Pic River, now out of class, was sold to Stratherne Terminals of Hamilton for scrap. Also retired that fall was the Shelter Bay which was sold to the Goderich Elevator and Transit Company as a grain storage barge. The Heron Bay was sent to Quebec City and eventually scrapped at Lauzon. The Helen Evans was laid up in Toronto and later sold to Stratherne Terminals for scrap.

The 1979 season saw another decrease in the tonnage operated by Q.&O.. In the fall Black River was sold to Marine Salvage who in turn resold her for off lakes use in the Caribbean. The Parker Evans, which was known as Marlhill, suffered boiler problems which forced her retirement during the fit-out for 1980.

Old age finally caught up with the steamer Lac Des Iles, the former Martha Hindman, in the fall of 1980. She was due for a hull survey but after being drydocked at Port Weller it became evident that the ship had sailed her last. The costs of replacing damaged plates could not be justified. She moved under her own power to Toronto where she was laid up.

In 1981 and 1982 the Q.&O. fleet numbered nine ships with the Baie Comeau II being sold late in 1982 leaving the company with eight vessels for what would be their last year of operation. Yet officials were somewhat optimistic on the future. However, the ever increasing canal tolls and high costs of operating the fleet proved to be the downfall of the Q.&O.. As 1983 began appointments were made for the entire fleet. They were as follows: Chicago Tribune: John Leonard Master, R. Schreiber Chief,

Franquelin: B. Wolstenholm Master, N. Purvis Chief, Golden Hind: Fred Bigham Master, J. Coates Chief, Lac Ste. Anne: W. Thoms Master, G. Doherty Chief, Meldrum Bay: L. Pulford Master, B. Given Chief, Outarde: E Sipila Master, B. Brissette Chief, New York News: E. Holden Master, P. Peloquin Chief, and Thorold: E. Penny Master, A. Williams Chief.

However, before the season started Lac Ste. Anne was held back in reserve. She was towed from her winter berth in Toronto to Hamilton as her dock was required by other ships in the former port. A total of 148 cargoes were carried that last season which included 123 types of grain or malt. The remainder were of ore, salt, coke, pig iron, pitch, ash, fertilizer, gypsum and quartzite.

BLACK RIVER on her last trip for Q.&O. headed for the scrapyard, October 1979 (Leonard LePage Photo)

A PAINFUL DECISION

On December 15, 1983, Robert Savage, President of Quebec and Ontario Transportation, announced that the shipping company would no longer operate after the close of the 1983 navigation season. At that point three of the eight ship fleet had already tied up with the remainder to finish their voyages and lay-up before the end of the month. Seasonal employees were given termination notices, some staff employees were offered early retirement and some were transferred within the corporation. However, other employees, unfortunately, were laid off at the end of the year.

Savage's announcement went on to say, "We are offering the Company's assets for sale. A group of Q. & O. employees have made a proposal to acquire some of the ships and we will be carrying out discussions with them. We would like to see the ships continue operating and will give preference to employees. At the same time we are seeking other interested buyers."

He further noted that the company had been operating at a loss and that they had been seeking partners for a joint venture or merger but were not successful. The possible improvement of the situation did not look encouraging and therefore the decision to close had to be made.

A letter to the Ministry of Labour in Ottawa notified

Robert W. Savage — final president of Q.&O. Transportation (Q.&O. files)

The fourth THOROLD sails in the Desgagnes fleet as CATHERINE DESGAGNES (SG)

them of the company's decision and gave notice of the termination of 190 employees classified in the occupations of admnistrative staff, captains, chief engineers, licensed and unlicensed ships crew. Terminations were to take place at terminals at Thunder Bay and Toronto plus the office located in St. Catharines.

A press release the following day included further information to the demise of the fleet which included the rise of fuel, labour and repair costs. Lockage fees on the Welland Canal also hurt the operators of small ships like the Q. & O.. It mentioned, "Our costs to use the canal have increased 300% since 1981. Small ships are charged the same fee as large bulk carriers with four times the cargo capacity."

On January 20, 1984, Quebec and Ontario Transportation Company Limited announced that it had sold its eight ship fleet to Le Groupe Desgagnes Inc., a Quebec based transportation and stevedoring firm. The purchase was ratified by the Board of Directors of the Groupe Desgagnes Inc. with terms of the sale not being disclosed. The ratification took place on January 24, two days after the Q. & O.'s 70th anniversary.

The men and the ships went different ways. Three ships were never to turn their wheel again. Another, after a brief re-entry in operation, was retired and today the four smaller ships remain part of the Desgagnes fleet. As for the personnel, some retired while others found positions with other shipping firms. The people who served the company were understandably upset by the loss of their positions but their loyalty, dedication and respect for the Quebec and Ontario Transportation Company throughout the years brought a sense of pride still echoed today.

The ships, officers and men of the Q. & O. are remembered with an anchor at Lock 3 on the Welland Ship Canal.

At the unveiling of the anchor on August 8, 1984, Robert M. Schmon, chairman of the parent Ontario Paper Company, noted that the anchor was from the Black River, one of the many ships that sailed under the Q. & O. flag on the inland waterway.

"These ships occupy a lasting place in the history of our Company. For many years they were the lifeline of our business.

"At Thorold we brought in wood and shipped out newsprint by water. The ships played an essential role in the construction of Baie Comeau and for years after, as all our newsprint had to be moved by ships.

"However, over time — and for a variety of reasons — it became more economical to transport both our raw materials and finished products by rail or truck. Still the fleet remained an important part of our overall operations until last year. To keep it competitive would have required massive amounts of money that we were unable to provide. Reluctantly we concluded there was no alternative but to withdraw from the shipping business.

"We feel a deep and personal loss with the passing of the Q. & O.; none feel it more than those who sailed the ships and those who managed the affairs of the fleet over the years. However, they should all experience a sense of satisfaction for a job well done."

Robert M. Schmon — Chairman of the Company (Q.&O. files)

John Houghton — President of Ontario Paper when Q.&O. ceased operations (Q.&O. files)

THE SHIPS OF THE Q.&O.

INTRODUCTION:

The Quebec and Ontario Transportation Company Limited, (Q.&O.) and its predecessor, the Ontario Transportation and Pulp Company Limited, (O.T. & P.) owned thirty-five different ships during the seventy seasons of service on the Great Lakes.

This section will relate the history of the company freighters and will not include such ships as Wiley M. Egan or Opco. The former, an old wooden freighter, was acquired to be sunk as a dock at Shelter Bay, Quebec. Unfortunately it broke up in the first storm.

The latter, a 110 foot (33.5 metre) World War One surplus subchaser, was later called the Mareuilendole and served as a dispatch boat on the St. Lawrence.

Identifying the company vessels was often a challenge. Some, particularly the earlier ships, retained the name they brought to the company. Others honoured areas where they traded.

Later names associated with geographical regions where the Ontario Paper Company had an interest.

Q.&O. had a habit of recycling vessel names. For example there were four different ships to sail as Thorold after the headquarters town of the Ontario Paper Company in Ontario.

Three company ships were called Outarde. They recognized Rivière-aux-Outardes (River of Geese) which provided a hydro-electric power source for company operations at Baie Comeau, Quebec.

There were also a trio of ships called New York News after the Tribune Company newspaper in New York.

Two ships were operated as Manicouagan, Franquelin, Heron Bay, Shelter Bay and Chicago Tribune.

There were similar names as well such as Joseph Medill and Joseph Medill Patterson plus Baie Comeau and Baie Comeau II. So at times, keeping track of names can be confusing.

The senior citizen among company ships lasted fifty-four seasons. It sailed briefly as the first Thorold but spent most of its career as the second Chicago Tribune.

In addition to the two fleet names, the O.T. & P. to 1933 and the Q.&O. Transportation, there were several subsidiaries. These included the Chicago Tribune Transportation Company, Comet Enterprises and Trico Enterprises.

Comet was established in 1962 when two older American lakers were acquired. It was based in Hamilton, Bermuda.

Trico Enterprises was set up as a subsidiary in 1972 but vessel operations for both remained in the Q.&O. office in Canada.

From a humble one ship operation, Q.&O. grew to a maximum of sixteen vessels in the 1978 season. That year they carried a record high of 321 cargoes for the season or an average of 20.1 payloads per ship.

Seventeen different commodities were carried that year. Shipments of ore accounted for almost 25% of all loads.

By 1983, the final year of operation, Q.&O. ran only seven ships and carried but 148 shipments. Season totals had declined annually since the summit of 1978.

The members of the fleet are listed in the order in which they were acquired. They are titled under the name or names used in company colours. When more than one name has been used their placement is identified by small Roman numerals. For example Outarde (ii) refers to the second ship named Outarde. A brief story on chartered vessels follows at the end of the fleet list.

HONOREVA, shown on the right passing Algonquin, eluded most photographers
(John Boyd Photo, J.H. Bascom Collection)

HONOREVA

Quebec and Ontario Transportation's forerunner was the Ontario Transportation and Pulp Company. It was incorporated in 1914 to bring supplies of pulpwood to Thorold for conversion to newsprint.

Still without timberlands of their own, the Ontario Paper Company purchased much of its wood from the Anticosti Island region of Quebec. The first vessel was chartered to bring the logs to Thorold and this was the Honoreva.

The ship was almost new having been built in 1913 by Osborne, Graham and Company of Sunderland, England. It measured 240 feet (73.2 metres) long and was registered at 1,452 gross tons. She was powered by a triple expansion engine of 17-28-46x33.

Honoreva was owned by the Donald Steamship Company and the charter arrangement carried an option to purchase.

She could carry 850 cords of pulpwood westbound and the new company arranged for Honoreva to haul coal as a downbound cargo. This was usually delivered to Montreal and the ship could handle 1,800 tons per trip.

The charter proved to be a good start for the Company. As a result Honoreva was purchased outright on August 17, 1916.

Actual ownership in the fleet was shortlived. There was a war on in Europe and Honoreva was sold for saltwater trading across the English Channel on August 24.

Although she only spent one week as an official part of the company fleet, her sale earned a tidy profit for Ontario Paper.

The new owners renamed the vessel Asturienne in 1916 but she was not to sail much longer. The company's first acquisition became a casualty of the war and was sent to the bottom in 1917 via enemy action.

TOILER

Needing a replacement vessel, O.T.&P. quickly invested their profit from the sale of Honoreva. They did not have to look far selecting Toiler, a vessel already in Great Lakes service.

This ship had been built on speculation by Swan, Hunter and Wigham Richardson at Newscastle, England. She was completed in 1910 and was unusual to be sure. Her engine was an internal explosive two-cycle diesel connected directly to the propeller. The fuel was stored in the double bottom instead of the usual ballast.

This experimental power plant was not a success and Toiler was converted to a steamer at Kingston during the winter of 1912-13. The new engine was a fore and aft compound, built in 1882, and had previously served in the D.C. Whitney.

Toiler carried coal from Newcastle to Calais, France, on her first trip and spent a number of months on saltwater.

On September 21, 1911, the vessel arrived at Montreal and was under charter to James Richardson. He purchased the ship in 1912 for the grain trade.

Toiler was acquired by O.T.&P. in 1916 for $90,706. She went to work in the pulpwood trade handling 1,000 cords per trip. This topped Honoreva by 150 cords. Col. McCormick immediately improved the sailors living conditions aboard ship by installing showers. These were still far from common aboard ships.

Canada Steamship Lines purchased this vessel in 1918 for $350,000 thus the company made a considerable profit but finding a replacement was a difficult task.

CSL renamed the ship Mapleheath a year later and the vessel still carries the name.

Her duties for CSL varied. She transported coal and grain much of the time but also brought pulpwood into the lakes.

Mapleheath made news on December 8, 1920, when she ran over her own anchor, was holed, and sank in the Gabriel Lock at Lachine, Quebec. She was raised and repaired at Kingston.

In 1929 another engine was installed. This was a triple expansion dating from 1903. It had previously served Simla. Then, in 1947, Mapleheath was reboiled.

CSL sent Mapleheath into Kingston for lay-up with the opening of the St. Lawrence Seaway in 1959. McAllister Towing purchased the ship and had it converted to a lighter. The pilot-house was removed and a crane mounted on deck.

Since then the vessel has been active on the St. Lawrence coming to the aid of ships which were aground. She was stationed at Kingston until recently but has since been moved to Montreal.

On numerous occasions tugs have brought Mapleheath to the scene of marine accidents where her crane unloaded the stranded ship. The tugs then proceeded to a safe anchorage and reloaded the salvaged vessel.

On one occasion, on November 27, 1978, Mapleheath herself went aground. She had lightered the Turkish freighter C. Mehmet on the St. Lawrence and was taking the salvaged cargo to Hamilton for discharge. Mapleheath broke loose and grounded off the Niagara River and, for a change, she was the one that had to be salvaged.

This sturdy hull, closing in on her 80th birthday, has served several owners well.

TOILER, underway in 1915, survives in the 80's as the barge Mapleheath
(Pesha photo, Q.&O. files)

MARY H. BOYCE

The third addition to the fleet in 1916 was the oak-hulled bulk carrier Mary H. Boyce. Like Middlesex, this had been a U.S. flag vessel.

Her construction had been undertaken in 1888 by Duncan Robertson at Grand Haven, Michigan. The ship was based there and served S.H. Boyce who named the ship after his wife.

Mary H. Boyce worked in the lumber trade on the Great Lakes. She was rebuilt on several occasions and, despite her age, was still a sound ship when acquired by O.T. & P.

She too went to work in the pulpwwod trade. Her 430-cord capacity was less than Toiler but towing the Middlesex, they served to augment the growing requirements of the company. She could also carry 800 tons of coal for downbound voyages.

After six seasons the Boyce was sold. New steel steamers were on the way and the ship passed to N.M. Paterson of Fort William. This firm was in the early stages of development and used the Boyce to pick up damp grain at other Lakehead elevators and take it to the Paterson elevator for drying. This was a successful operation. Occasionally the company sent the Boyce to Georgian Bay with a full load of grain.

Mary H. Boyce caught fire at Fort William in 1928 and was badly damaged. Repairs were not worthwhile but the hull remained until being towed into Lake Superior and scuttled in deep water off Isle Royale in 1936.

MARY H. BOYCE served in the pulpwood trade (Q.&O. files)

MIDDLESEX

Middlesex was another addition to the fleet in 1916. She was a wooden schooner barge and her service was of short duration.

This vessel dated from 1880 and was constructed at St. Clair, Michigan. The ship had been built for the lumber trade with a capacity of 770,000 board feet and it sailed for several U.S. flag owners. These included the Sopher Lumber Co., J.A. Calbick, and Henry Brock.

Middlesex was 198 feet long. (60.35 metres) Tonnage was registered at 618 gross.

The vessel came under Canadian registry for O.T. & P. in 1916 and operated briefly between the St. Lawrence and Thorold.

Middlesex broke loose of the MARY H. BOYCE on August 13, 1917, while downbound on the Upper St. Lawrence. She stranded on Rapide Plat and was abandoned to the insurers ending her brief service to the company.

Sin-Mac Lines Ltd., a salvage firm, purchased the hull and had it refloated. They took the remains to Sorel and, in 1918, had it rebuilt as Woodlands. The ship then worked on the St. Lawrence into the mid-twenties and it was scrapped in 1929.

The barge MIDDLESEX operated until running aground (Milwaukee Public Library)

LINDEN filled in after World War One (Pesha photo, Q.&O. files)

LINDEN

Replacing the Toiler in 1918 was not an easy task despite the profit earned by her sale. Due to the war few ships were available and the best O.T. & P. could acquire was Linden.

Unfortunately Linden was older, wood hulled and of less capacity, handling only 571 cords of pulpwood per trip.

Linden had been built by Jenks Shipbuilding of Port Huron, Michigan and launched December 15, 1894. When she began trading the next season Linden concentrated in the copper trade between Lake Linden, Michigan, and Black Rock, New York. She also worked in the lumber trade and had a capacity of 900,000 board feet.

On June 23, 1905, Linden went to the bottom of the St. Clair River after a collision with the City of Rome. The latter also sank and two lives were lost in the incident.

Linden was patched, pumped out and repaired. She

worked for a number of more years before joining O.T. & P.

This vessel joined the pulpwood trade to Thorold but this was not without the occasional problem. Once, during a storm, she ran low on fuel and had to burn part of the wood cargo to keep steam up. This was not good for profits.

Another time Linden failed to go into reverse entering one of the locks of the Third Welland Canal. She crashed through the gates and caused considerable damage.

As the company woodlands opened up on the lower St. Lawrence Linden and Mary H. Boyce were the prime ships for moving the wood out of Franquelin and Shelter Bay.

Linden was sold in 1923 with the arrival of the new ships from overseas. R. Burns of Detroit operated the ship briefly but it burned at the Lake Huron port of Tawas City on November 28, 1923. The hull remained until removal in 1930.

CHICAGO TRIBUNE (i) / THOROLD (ii)

Clearly the Mary H. Boyce and Linden were not adequate to supply the growing needs of the Thorold mill. Second hand tonnage was not available and frequently the parent Ontario Paper Company had to charter vessels. This was not the best economics as freight rates continued to climb higher.

To solve this problem two new steel freighters were ordered and these would be able to carry larger cargoes at lower costs. They could handle 1,100 cords of pulpwood or over 2,000 tons of coal. Their arrival led to the sale of the Boyce and Linden.

Chicago Tribune was chosen as the name for one of the ships and she was built by Swan, Hunter and Wigham Richardson at Wallsend, England, and measured 258 feet (78.6 metres) in overall length. Her tonnage was registered at 1,689 gross and 987 net. An 800 horsepower triple expansion engine provided adequate power for the lakes and river trades.

The vessel crossed the Atlantic and began trading in the late summer of 1922 bringing pulpwood from the St. Lawrence.

Operation of the ships on the busy lakes and rivers, often limited by confining channels, often caused navigational problems. These, combined with unpredictable weather, challenged the most experienced Captains. Few ships escaped without the occasional difficulty.

Chicago Tribune was not immune. She was in collision on July 29, 1928, while upbound across Lake St. Louis on the St. Lawrence. Also involved was the British deep sea freighter Elfstone.

A few years later, on August 8, 1932, Chicago Tribune ran aground on the St. Lawrence on a uniquely named outcropping of rock called Jackass Shoal. The ship was bound for Thorold with pulpwood at the time.

Despite these minor setbacks, Chicago Tribune was a successful hauler of pulpwood and received additional cargo gear to make loading and unloading operations more efficient.

When O.T.&P. was reorganized in 1933 as the Quebec and Ontario Transportation Company (hereafter referred to as Q.&O.) several ships were renamed to reflect more on their activities. As a result this wood-carrying ship became the Thorold in recognition of her common port of discharge.

Thorold concentrated in similar trade patterns until 1940. War was again raging in Europe and vessels were in short supply. This ship was requisitioned for deep sea trading and left Canada in June 1940 with a cargo of saw logs for Great Britain.

It was intended to operate Thorold between Wales and France carrying coal. On August 22, 1940, during the first cross channel trip, Thorold encountered Nazi aircraft and came under attack. The vessel was bombed, hit by gunfire and sunk 2-1/2 miles south of Smalls, England. There were eleven lives lost in the attack but fortunately thirteen of the crew were rescued.

The original CHICAGO TRIBUNE upbound with pulpwood (Ken Lowes Collection)

Later CHICAGO TRIBUNE carried a billboard advertising "Liberty" magazine (J.H. Bascom photo)

From 1933, until her loss on the Atlantic, THOROLD brought pulpwood to her namesake port (Q.&O. files)

NEW YORK NEWS (i) / SHELTER BAY (i)

The second addition in 1922 was also built overseas. She too was named for one of the parent company newspapers and thus went to work as New York News.

The North of Ireland Shipbuilding Company of Londonderry constructed this ship for O.T.&P. Her dimensions and capacity were similar to Chicago Tribune and she also carried an 800 horsepower triple expansion engine.

New York News joined the pulp and coal trades and proved to be an excellent addition to the fleet.

A severe storm lashed the Gulf of St. Lawrence in late October 1926 and several vessels became casualties. New York News was at Shelter Bay to load when the storm struck. In time she broke her moorings in the violent weather. The vessel was driven aground in the climatic upheaval and, as she had no radio, was out of contact with shore personnel. Fearing the worst, New York News was, for a time, reported lost. But she fared better than others including A.D. MacTier of the Hall fleet which became a total loss.

Salvage experts removed New York News from her rocky perch and, after repairs by Davie Shipbuilding at Lauzon, Quebec, she was sent back to work.

In 1933 this ship became the Shelter Bay for Q.&O. and continued to wear a path to Thorold with loads of wood.

Shelter Bay saw some saltwater service during war but was much more fortunate than her old running mate Thorold.

Over the years Shelter Bay received a new pilot house, masts and cargo booms and proved to be a good carrier.

On April 28, 1956, Captain Geoffrey Hawthorn, a former Q.&O. Captain, began writing a column in the St. Catharines Standard called "Ships That Ply The Lakes." This weekly feature, taken over by Skip Gillham after the Captain's death, has been a fixture in the Niagara area paper ever since and Captain Hawthorn's first story recounted the history of Shelter Bay.

The vessel's career was nearing an end when he wrote but one last chapter remained. Recognizing the inevitable changes in Great Lakes trnsportation resulting from the development of the Seaway, Q.&O. sold Shelter Bay to N.M. Paterson and Sons Limited in 1958. They renamed her Labradoc.

Service proved to be brief and Labradoc went in to retirement at Kingston after the 1959 season.

One last trip remained and in August 1961 a tug was dispatched to bring the vessel to Port Dalhousie along the Third Welland Canal. There the old New York News/Shelter Bay was soon reduced to scrap.

NEW YORK NEWS upbound in the Welland Canal (Sykes collection)

A storm in 1926 put NEW YORK NEWS on the rocks of the St. Lawrence (James Roberts photo)

The vessel was renamed SHELTER BAY in 1933 (W.E. Shore photo, Q.&O. files)

The last few years were spent as LABRADOC (Pete Worden photo)

THOROLD (i) / CHICAGO TRIBUNE (ii)

Rail rates for newsprint, continued to climb in the 1920's. Col. McCormick was convinced that water transportation would be feasible with the proper ship and commissioned a research and design project. A thorough investigation was carried out before Earles Shipbuilding and Engineering of Hull, England, was contracted to build what became the motor ship Thorold.

This vessel was able to haul 3,000 tons per trip, roughly the ten day output of the Thorold mill. A trunk deck was added to increase capacity over standard canal ships. Stabilizer tanks were included in the construction to lower the vessel's centre of gravity and a Sulzer Air Blast Injection diesel engine was selected as it required less space in the engine room.

The 258.5 foot (78.9 metre) vessel was an immediate success. She carried double the paper payload of similarly sized ships.

During 1931, her first full season on the job, Thorold hauled 68,562 tons of newsprint on twenty-three trips. Improved loading, unloading and storage practices were developed and the railways lost a customer.

In 1933 the vessel was renamed Chicago Tribune to reflect its role in supplying newsprint to that paper. This was also the year that the fleet was reorganized as the Quebec and Ontario Transportation Company.

Chicago Tribune remained in the newsprint trade for many years but she also handled other cargoes on occasion. This was especially true in later years as other vessels joined her in the newsprint run.

Efficiency was upgraded. First, in 1958, she was repowered with a Fairbanks-Morse diesel engine. Then, in 1962, Chicago Tribune was lengthened to 319 feet (97.2 metres) overall in work at Port Weller Drydocks in St. Catharines, Ont. The vessel could now carry close to 5,000 tons in the post-Seaway era.

By the early seventies other cargoes had to be found. In 1968, for example, fifteen of the Tribune's twenty-one cargoes were newsprint. The remainder were corn.

During her final sixteen seasons for Q.&O. Chicago Tribune carried 363 payloads. Mixed grain led all commodities accounting for 82 shipments or 22.5 per cent. Newsprint fell to 20.1% but none of these came out of

THOROLD is seen arriving at Montreal in 1930 (Ken Lowes Collection)

CHICAGO TRIBUNE approaches the Glendale Bridge on the Welland Canal on September 19, 1976 (SG)

Thorold after 1972. Rail transportation was again the chief means of moving paper to Chicago.

On a few occasions Chicago Tribune was on the St. Lawrence and she brought newsprint upbound out of Baie Comeau for the presses of the namesake newspaper.

Although designed to carry newsprint, this vessel was forced to prove her versatility. Other cargoes had to be sought and Chicago Tribune proved she could carry various grains, salt, clay, pig iron, steel, pitch, coal and even a small load of concrete pipe as the need arose.

Thunder Bay now became the chief loading centre as 56.3% of all cargoes in the final sixteen years originated there. Toronto, recipient of 44.1% of the cargoes, was the prime discharge port. Prescott, Goderich, Duluth, Collingwood and Sorel were also important among the twenty-three different stops for unloading.

During the 1983 season, the final one for Q.&O., Chicago Tribune carried but nineteen cargoes. Most were barley or malt-barley from Thunder Bay to Toronto. The only exception was a split load of wheat and oats divided between elevators at Collingwood and Goderich. When the ship tied up at Toronto in late December she had carried her last for Q.&O.

Transport Desgagnes put Chicago Tribune to work in 1984 and she continued to trade on their account until the end of the 1985 season. The ship made but one trip, Thunder Bay to Toronto, in 1986 before laying up. At this writing she remains idle at Toronto although she had been used to store soy beans in 1987.

Despite her many years in lakes service, this ship has had very few problems. There was a collision September 29, 1960, with Shenango II in the St. Clair Flats off Marysville, Michigan. Damage was above the waterline for the grain laden Tribune.

On September 2, 1975, Chicago Tribune went aground in Georgian Bay while hauling grain to Collingwood. A total of 30,000 bushels had to be lightered to the Charles W. Johnson before the vessel would float free.

Later, on July 26, 1984, another grounding occurred. This was in the Middle Neebish Channel below the Soo Locks. This time pumping ballast released the vessel.

Chicago Tribune holds the record for longevity in the fleet as she put in fifty-four years in company colours. Her design proved the faith of Col. McCormick and the wisdom of the marine architects. If business conditions improve she may yet sail again.

NEW YORK NEWS (ii)

Soon the production of newsprint at the Thorold mill exceeded the needs of the Tribune at Chicago. The excess paper could be shipped to New York for the News and several routes were scrutinized.

Water transportation, via the New York State Barge canal, offered some advantages but the low bridges and ballasting problems limited cargo capacity. Once the railways realized they could control the market, the rates went up.

Q.&O. needed a ship that could sail from Thorold to New York and still carry a decent payload through the fourteen foot draft of the St. Lawrence Canals. Due to the Depression many ships were laid up and available.

The Belvoir was selected and purchased in June 1933 for $95,000. Renamed New York News, she had good cubic capacity and could carry 2,400 tons of paper per trip from Thorold to New York. Upbound, on the return trip, she hauled pulpwood.

This ship had been built as Belvoir by Swan, Hunter and Wigham Richardson at Wallsend, England, in 1925. She was designed for the International Waterways Navigation Company and spent nine seasons in their colours.

As New York News, she carried newsprint in 1933 and 1934 and her success resulted in the railways reducing their rates to New York. New work was found for the ship.

This was one of the Canadian vessels requisitioned by the government during World War Two. Some served in British coastal trades while others worked the rivers of South America in the bauxite trade. New York News' service was less glamourous. Wearing a wartime grey hull, the vessel was operated by the United States Maritime Commission on the Atlantic from late 1942 until May 9, 1943.

Her main work was concentrated on taking supplies to the air base at Goose Bay, Labrador, and bringing coal from Norfolk, Virginia, to Boston, Massachussetts.

NEW YORK NEWS passes up the old canals of the St. Lawrence (Q.&O. files)

NEW YORK NEWS is drydocked at Montreal for a regular survey (Hayward Studios, Q.&O. files)

Most ships travelled in convoy through these dangerous waters as lone freighters were ideal targets for prowling U-boats. New York News had a close call in August 1942 off Matane, Quebec, while on convoy duty. The ship directly ahead was hit by a torpedo and sank with a serious loss of life. The News was shaken by the explosion but emerged unscathed.

New York News returned to Q.&O. to carry pulpwood, some newsprint, coal and grain. On December 13, 1948, she stranded on a shoal in the St. Lawrence Narrows and sustained damage that required drydocking at Kingston, Ont.

This vessel operated for Q.&O. through 1962 and passed down the Welland Canal for the last time on November 29 of that year. She was sold to Buckport Shipping Ltd. and renamed Buckport for service on the St. Lawrence.

This venture was of short duration and the vessel was scrapped at Montreal in 1965 by St. Lawrence Iron and Metal Ltd.

JOSEPH MEDILL

Undoubtedly the saddest moment in the history of Q.&O. Transportation occurred in 1935 with the loss of the new bulk carrier Joseph Medill. It had left England for Great Lakes service and just never arrived.

The "Great Depression" had gripped the world in the Thirties and shipping was among the many industries that suffered. Several fleets went into bankruptcy yet Q.&O. risked capital to order a much needed ship to haul pulpwood from Shelter Bay and Franquelin on the Gulf of St. Lawrence to the parent company's mill at Thorold.

The new vessel was carefully designed. It was to carry record cargoes through the fourteen-foot draft limits of the St. Lawrence canals and would use the relatively new all-welded type of construction.

Named Joseph Medill, this ship would honour the founding editor of the Chicago Tribune newspaper.

In addition to carrying pulpwood, the vessel had large hatches for loading newsprint and smooth surfaces in the holds to minimize damage.

Q.&O. decided to use twin diesel engines instead of steam power. This reduced the vessel's weight and the size of the engineroom and thus increased the amount of cargo space available. Yes, Joseph Medill would be an efficient ship.

Swan, Hunter and Wigham Richardson were contracted to build the vessel and it was launched on July 4, 1935. Joseph Medill was the largest vessel of welded construction yet to be built and it measured 259 feet (78.94 metres) in overall length and had a beam of 45 feet, 10 inches (13.36 metres).

Company officials attended the launching ceremony and oversaw a successful sea trial. The vessel was to be a money maker from the start and loaded 2,784 tons of Scotch anthracite coal for delivery to Montreal. On August 10 the ship cleared Leith, Scotland, for the transatlantic run.

Unfortunately, somewhere on the Atlantic, Joseph Medill went down. It was last seen August 17 by a Norwegian passenger ship and shortly afterwards a severe storm struck the area. The vessel vanished without a trace and the entire crew was lost.

JOSEPH MEDILL was launched on July 4, 1935 (courtesy George Corbin)

JOSEPH MEDILL is ready for launching at Wallsend (courtesy George Corbin)

FRANQUELIN (i)

Although some speculated that the loss of the Joseph Medill was due to the all-welded construction Q.&O. did not waiver from the new technology. They had faith in their design, their tests and their builder and once again ordered a similar ship.

The only change from the Joseph Medill design was increased support for the hatch covers. Swan, Hunter and Wigham Richardson again built the ship and this one was launched as Franquelin.

On May 16, 1936, nine months after Joseph Medill sank, the replacement cleared England for Montreal carrying a cargo of clay.

Franquelin was a busy ship and soon proved the value of its design carrying 1,360 cords of pulpwood per trip. Other commodities were also hauled and the vessel set St. Lawrence canal records with 3,330 tons of coal and 120,109 bushels of corn.

Franquelin, and other company ships, played a key role in the construction of the town of Baie Comeau, the paper mill and hydro plants as well as supplying the needs of the woods camps. Franquelin regularly delivered coal to feed the mill boilers before they were converted to electricity. In addition, she had two large tanks on deck that were loaded with diesel fuel at Montreal for downbound deliveries.

Construction material, prefabricated steel out of Dominion Bridge at Lachine and heavy machinery headed for the site by ship. Even hay had to be brought in for the era when the woods department used horses.

The ship continued through the end of the Depression, the war years and the industrial development after the war. Other shipping companies began to build all-welded and diesel powered canallers and Franquelin remained competitive with the best of them.

The ship survived the early years of the St. Lawrence Seaway and was sold in 1964.

North Shore Shipping Ltd. purchased Franquelin and it served on the St. Lawrence as Prince Ungava. On occasion it visited the Great Lakes in bulk trades.

Then, in 1967, Desgagnes Navigation acquired the ship and named it Jean Talon. Service again combined lakes and St. Lawrence runs.

On May 3, 1974, however, Canadian registry was closed as the ship was sold Panamanian. Balboa Navigation S.A. bought the vessel and renamed it Sovereign Opal.

The former Franquelin now left the Great Lakes for the last time. The new service was on the Gulf of Mexico and among the West Indies. It worked in this trade for over a year but laid up at Mobile, Alabama, late in 1975.

Rose Bay Shipping, another Panamanian concern, purchased the ship early in 1976 and it cleared for Antigua February 6. Renamed Falcon III, it was noted to be trading on the Black Sea in July 1976 and in April 1977 was reported bound for the Suez Canal.

There the trail of the former company ship evaporates. Perhaps it was bound for one of the many scrapyards in India or Pakistan and the dismantling of the hull was not reported.

Forty years of successful trading on the Great Lakes, Gulf of Mexico and across the Atlantic to the Black Sea had certainly justified the faith in the design developed by Q.&O. in the depths of the Depression.

FRANQUELIN set many cargo records on the St. Lawrence (Pete Worden photo)

After leaving Q.&O. this ship sailed under several names including PRINCE UNGAVA (Ted Jones photo)

HERON BAY (i)

The purchase of Heron Bay in 1939 marked a new step in company operations. The ship was acquired on December 2, 1939, and renamed for service the following year.

To this point all of the company ships could trade through the St. Lawrence canals. After all the fleet was established to haul pulpwood from the St. Lawrence to Thorold.

Timber operations on Lake Superior were now in full swing and a larger ship could handle bigger payloads as it would be free of the confining St. Lawrence locks.

The Heron Bay was named for a village on the north shore of Lake Superior. The Ontario Paper Company had logging operations in that area and Heron Bay was the centre of these operations.

The ship could carry 2,700 tons of newsprint in the cargo holds and this later topped 3,000 tons when the company developed a method of carrying rolls of paper on deck. The ship was also able to bring 2,000 cords of pulpwood to the Thorold mill.

This bulk carrier had been built as a barge. It was the second vessel constructed by the Collingwood Shipbuilding Company of Collingwood, Ontario, and followed the passenger ship Huronic from the Georgian Bay shipyard.

Christened Agawa, the vessel was launched July 19, 1902, for the Algoma Central and Hudson Bay Railway. It went into service in the grain trade and was usually towed by the steamer Monkshaven. The latter, however, was wrecked in 1905.

Algoma returned Agawa to Collingwood in 1907 and had it rebuilt as a steamer. It emerged as 390 feet (118.9 metres) long and powered by a triple expansion engine.

Agawa usually ran into Georgian Bay ports and was enroute on December 7, 1927, when it grounded on Advance Reef off Manitoulin Island. The ship was abandoned to the insurers.

The famous Reid Wrecking Company released the vessel May 16, 1928, and had it rebuilt at Collingwood.

Arrow Steamships Ltd. acquired the vessel on June 10, 1929, and it operated in association with Toronto Elevators as the Robert P. Durham. The ship frequently unloaded at Toronto but was idle there from time to time during the depression.

Q.&O. had Heron Bay carry newsprint, grain and pulpwood. It too was needed to aid the war effort and was ordered to haul iron ore between U.S. ports in 1942—43. This would normally be the domain of American vessels but Heron Bay was needed and carried 52,737 tons in 1942 alone.

The sixteen Maritime Class vessels were built by the United States Maritime Commission in 1943 so Heron Bay was released and returned to Q.&O. The new bulk carriers had a total one trip capacity of over a quarter million tons of ore.

Heron Bay continued to operate for Q.&O. for almost twenty years. Its last run down the Welland canal occurred November 29, 1962, and the ship headed for the St. Lawrence and a new duty.

Federal Commerce and Navigation purchased Heron Bay for salt storage at Baie Comeau. Renamed Federal Husky, it was useful into 1963 but then remained empty and idle to 1965.

Sold via the Commonwealth Metal Company to Cia Espagnol de Demolicione Naval, the Heron Bay was towed to Bilbao, Spain. It arrived November 26, 1965, and was soon scrapped.

On June 12, 1985, an old anchor from Heron Bay was unveiled at the Battle of Beaverdams Park at Thorold honouring the 140th Anniversary of the Second Welland Canal. The event was sponsored by the City of Thorold and the Ontario Paper Company.

AGAWA was built as a barge and is shown at Midland in 1904 (J.W. Bald photo, Ken Lowes Collection)

ROBERT P. DURHAM upbound at Sault St. Marie (Gillham Collection)

HERON BAY is seen at the Johnstown Elevator on November 11, 1954 (Dan McCormick photo)

OUTARDE (i)

Q.&O. purchased the steamer Brulin in 1939. This vessel was already fifteen years old and had had an eventful career.

It had been built by Palmer's Shipbuilding and Iron Company at Hebburn-on-Tyne, U.K. in 1924 for the Montreal Forwarding Company.

The 261 foot (79.6 metre) freighter ran aground near Kingston on October 15, 1932. The ship struck Melville Shoal while downbound for Montreal with a load of grain. The vessel required the assistance of tugs to float free.

Later, on November 16, 1936, the crew spotted the abandoned tanker barge Bruce Hudson adrift on Lake Ontario. The pulling tug had to leave it to go for fuel and Brulin towed the hull to Port Weller. Salvage fees totalling $9,999 were later awarded.

Q.&O. renamed the Brulin as Outarde. The company liked the fact that it could sail with a nineteen foot draft

on the upper lakes. This allowed a substantial payload and the ship went to work on a triangular route.

Clearing Thorold with newsprint, Outarde would sail to Chicago to unload. There it often took on coal or grain and, after delivery, proceeded to the Lake Superior port of Heron Bay to receive a shipment of pulpwood for Thorold.

The Canadian Government requisitioned Outarde in 1942 and the ship went into the east coast coal trade on loan to the United States Maritime Commission. It would load at Norfolk, and Hampton Roads, Virginia, and sail to Boston, Massachusetts, staying on the Inland Channel as much as possible in order to avoid contact with the dreaded U-Boats.

While north the vessel occasionally loaded newsprint at Baie Comeau. In January 1943 Outarde ran aground on a shoal off the Gulf of St. Lawrence islands of St. Pierre

BRULIN sailed for Carter-Wood before joining Q.&O. (Ken Lowes Collection)

OUTARDE was a valuable addition to the fleet (Ken Lowes Collection)

and Miquelon. It was enroute to St. John's, Newfoundland, at the time and some cargo had to be dumped overboard to allow Outarde to float free.

On June 13, 1943, Outarde returned to Q.&O. but was in trouble again just after the war ended.

With the 1945 navigation season drawing to a close the upbound Outarde docked at Clayton, New York, on November 30 to take on fuel for the last run of the season to Thorold.

A late fall storm was whipping up Lake Ontario and when Outarde docked it struck a protruding rail with such force that the hull was punctured below the water line. Soon the ship was on the bottom for the winter.

An early attempt to raise the ship failed but in April 1946 Outarde was again afloat. The hull had been cofferdamed and pumped out and was then taken to Kingston for repairs.

There would be fifteen more good years for Outarde in Q.&O. colours. Late in its career the vessel received a new pilot-house, a larger squared model, but otherwise the ship changed little.

In 1960 Buckport Shipping Ltd. purchased this ship and renamed it James J. Buckler for service on the St. Lawrence.

It did not last long for on June 13, 1960, the former company ship stranded on Red Islet near the mouth of the Saguenay River. Three days later it sank during an unsuccessful salvage attempt. It remains on the bottom to this day.

A late season accident put OUTARDE on the bottom at Clayton, N.Y. (courtesy John Christopher)

Another view of OUTARDE on the bottom at Clayton, N.Y. (Gilham collection)

OUTARDE with a new pilothouse (SG)

COLABEE

War imposed severe limits on private shipping companies. Q.&O. remembered the difficulty in obtaining ships during World War One and hoped to avoid a similar problem.

Paper production from the Baie Comeau mill was supplying the needs of the New York News but to 1940 the cargo was transported there in chartered vessels.

In 1939 the Norwegian motorship Brand was chartered for five years but it was soon requisitioned for war service.

Thus in May 1940 the Tribune Company used corporate reorganization to reestablish the old Tonawanda Paper Company as the Michigan Atlantic Corporation. This allowed the operation of a vessel under the American flag. The company's name was soon changed to the Illinois Atlantic Corporation and they were able to purchase the Colabee.

This vessel was already old by deep sea standards. But in wartime such things did not matter.

The ship had been built at Portsmouth, New Hampshire, in 1920 for the United States Maritime Commission as Pagasset.

It later passed to a private concern on condition that it only be used in Atlantic coastal service.

This restriction was later lifted for Illinois Atlantic, for a fee, and Colabee could carry general cargo on transatlantic runs during the winter months.

Colabee was intended for service in the newsprint trade and was a success. The ship carried 5,100 tons of newsprint in the hold and was the first freighter to experiment with deck-loads of paper covered with tarpaulins. This increased the carrying capacity by 700 tons and the idea was soon used on other members of the fleet and eventually the whole industry.

Unfortunately, in January 1942, Colabee was called to battle under requisition by the United States Maritime Commission. The ship very nearly became a war casualty.

On March 12, 1942, Colabee cleared Nevitas, Cuba, with a cargo of sugar and was attacked by a submarine. A torpedo inflicted serious damage and the vessel was ordered abandoned.

This was a mistake. Many of the crew lost their lives in needless fashion as Colabee held together and did not sink.

Instead the ship was towed back to Nevitas, unloaded and taken to Tampa, Florida for repairs. The vessel was soon back in service and did not return to the company fleet until 1945.

Colabee resumed the newsprint run from Baie Comeau to New York for five years but the operation could not compete with lower rates available from foreign ships.

As a result Colabee was laid up late in 1949 and sold June 28, 1950, to owners based in San Francisco, California.

COLABEE carried newsprint to New York (Gillham Collection)

MANICOUAGAN (i) / WASHINGTON TIMES HERALD / MANITOULIN

Several fleets suffered multiple losses during the war. Their canal-sized vessels were really not suited for deep sea runs concentrating in areas that were dangerous waters.

Some canallers were used on the bauxite trade out of South America, some sailed along the Atlantic coast and some worked around the coast of the United Kingdom and across the English Channel to Europe. Q.&O. had suffered but one casualty, the Thorold (ii).

As a postwar replacement Q.&O. purchased a ship that had previous service on the Great Lakes and survived the war.

This vessel was similar to other company carriers. It had been built, on speculation, by Swan, Hunter and Wigham Richardson at Sunderland, England. The 261 foot (79.6 metre) vessel came to the Great Lakes where St. Lawrence Steamships were the successful bidders. This firm was a Canadian subsidiary of E.S. Crosby & Co. of Buffalo. The vessel was originally named Imari but this was changed to Delaware in 1931.

The British War Ministry requisitioned Delaware in 1940 for saltwater service. They brought the 2,313 gross ton freighter to England where it was operated as a collier by Wm. Cory and Son Ltd.

In 1943 the ship was renamed Empire Rother and a year later served as a tank carrier for the invasion of Europe.

After the war it continued in coastal service but was sold to Q.&O. on October 18, 1948.

Following an extensive refit this ship returned to the Great Lakes in June 1949 bearing the name Manicouagan.

The Tribune Company had added a third newspaper, the Washington Times Herald, in 1949. The vessel was thus renamed in 1951 to recognize the new paper's name. But it did not sail long as Washington Times Herald.

During the 1954 season the ship became Manitoulin, its sixth name, and continued to work in newsprint, pulp and other bulk tades.

Manitoulin was retired to Thorold in November 1960 and towed to Port Weller the following May. The ship was sold to A. Newman for scrap in August 1961 and towed to Port Dalhousie to be broken up.

This ship had served the company for only twelve years but carried three names and helped fill the post war gap in transportation needs.

IMARI
DELAWARE (1931)
EMPIRE ROTHER (1943)
MANICOUAGAN (1949)
WASHINGTON TIMES
     HERALD (1951)
MANITOULIN (1954)

MANICOUAGAN joined the fleet after World War Two (Q.&O. files)

48

WASHINGTON TIMES HERALD at Rapide du Plat on May 30, 1952 (Dan McCormick photo)

MANITOULIN was scrapped at Port Dalhousie
(The Standard, St. Catharines, Ont.)

The third name in company colours was MANITOULIN (Q.&O. files)

BLACK RIVER

Black River, which began service for Q.&O. as a barge, lasted thirty years in company colours. Most, however, were as a diesel powered freighter.

This was originally a consort barge built by F.W. Wheeler and Company of West Bay City, Michigan, in 1896. It was 366 feet (111.6 metres) long and operated for the Bessemer Steamship Company, the Pittsburgh Steamship Company and then the Marine Iron and Shipbuilding Company as the Sir Isaac Lothian Bell.

The early years concentrated in the ore trade but the ship likely hauled other commmodities on occasion.

In 1937 the Pigeon River Timber Company renamed the vessel as Blanche H. and it later served Lakehead Transportation plus the Great Lakes Lumber and Shipping Company in the lumber trade on the upper lakes.

On joining Q.&O. in 1949 the vessel was soon renamed as Black River in recognition of a river in a timber area north of Lake Superior. The ship worked in the pulpwood trade pulled by Rocky River.

It was soon determined that Black River would be more effective under its own power. Accordingly, the ship was taken to Port Weller Drydocks in St. Catharines, Ontario, and rebuilt as a dieselized bulk carrier.

Black River returned to service on October 20, 1952, as a 373 foot (113.7 metre) freighter with tonnage registered at 3,587 gross tons and 2,483 net tons. It could handle 5,400 tons deadweight, close to 200,000 bushels of grain or 2,100 cords of pulpwood.

The vessel's engine dated from 1931. It was a Burnmeister and Wain diesel, one of two salvaged from the sunken deep sea ship England. The other engine was installed in Pic River.

Black River managed six cargoes before the end of the 1952 season. Three were grain, two newsprint and one of coal. It was just the start of a busy new career.

In the years under diesel power Black River hauled 709 payloads for Q.&O. and these included thirty different commodities.

The most popular was newsprint and this was carried 26.9 per cent of the time. The ship loaded these cargoes every year but 1978. The peak season for newsprint was 1961 when fourteen were carried among the thirty-two payloads.

Pulpwood was the second most common cargo accounting for 11.1 per cent of all shipments. Little pulpwood was carried after 1964 and none after 1972.

The following averaged at least one cargo per year during her twenty-eight seasons. They are listed in descending order and include grain, coal, soybeans, corn, wheat, salt, clay and pig iron. Lesser, but still significant, amounts of pitch, steel and barley were also carried.

Thorold was the most popular loading port and ranked second among the discharge ports thanks to the many loads of newsprint and pulpwood.

Chicago, which placed third as a loading port, (coal and various grains) ranked first among the discharge centres due to the need for newsprint.

The Canadian Lakehead, now known as Thunder Bay, was the top loading port in later years and took second place overall.

Interestingly Baie Comeau, which was not visited prior to 1962 for loading and Heron Bay, where the ship did not call after 1963, ranked fourth and fifth respectively.

Sorel, Detroit, Erie, Ashtabula and Windsor rounded out the top ten among the forty-four different loading ports.

Among the centres where Black River loaded but once included major ports such as Duluth, Toronto, Kingston and Quebec City plus smaller centres like Spanish, Britt, Buffington and Sodus Point.

Black River averaged twenty-six cargoes a year over this period. The busiest season was 1956 when thirty-four shipments were handled while the quietest, after the first year, was 1974. There were eleven cargoes that latter season. The ship spent eight weeks at Port Weller Drydocks that summer for repairs and certification.

After the top three discharge ports came Prescott, Quebec City, Montreal, Baie Comeau, Hamilton, Goderich and Duluth. There appears to be no port that the ship visited to unload in each of its twenty-eight years.

Black River served a total of forty-six different discharge ports and stopped but once at eight of them.

BLACK RIVER began company service as a barge (W.E. Shore photo, Q.&O. files)

BLACK RIVER was rebuilt at Port Weller Drydocks (W.E. Shore photo, Q.&O. files)

While newsprint, coal, grain and pulpwood dominated the early work, Q.&O. personnel kept busy finding diverse cargoes for Black and Pic in later years.

The vessel benefitted from a ninety day certificate extension in July 1979 and managed twenty-two cargoes that last year and thirteen were different commodities.

Salt out of Windsor/Ojibway for Duluth was the most popular payload and this accounted for four shipments.

The last shipment of newsprint aboard this old paper carrier proved to be 3,677 metric tonnes. It loaded at Baie Comeau September 15 and was divided between Milwaukee and Chicago.

The last actual load for was Q.&O. 5,771 metric tonnes of pitch. It cleared Detroit October 9, 1979, for Baie Comeau and when the vessel returned up the Welland Canal on October 22 the destination was Ramey's Bend at Port Colborne. There the scrap firm of Marine Salvage tucked the vessel into their yard to await what most thought was the breaker's torch.

Incredibly, the scrap plans were put on hold and Black River won a reprieve. Cayman Shipping Corporation came north, checked the ship over and purchased the vessel for service out of U.S. Gulf Coast ports.

The navigation season was drawing to an end and a crew came aboard and had the ship ready by November 22. When it left the lakes it was sailing as the Tuxpancliffe.

A few years in the grain trade remained for this vessel despite being past its eightieth birthday.

On March 24, 1983, Tuxpancliffe was seized by U.S. Marshal's at Houston, Texas, to pay debts that included $153,000 in back pay and $53,000 in dockage fees.

The ship was ordered sold at auction but the high bid of $2,200 was considered inadequate and was set aside by a judge.

Finally, on September 3, 1983, Tuxpancliffe was sold for scrap via Marshal's sale bringing a reported $60,000.

The final voyage cleared Houston in October 1983 and the ship was delivered to Corpus Christi, Texas, to be scrapped.

An old Black River anchor, a spare that did not go south, was unveiled in a ceremony, sponsored by the Ontario Paper Company, the St. Lawrence Seaway, and the Welland Canals Foundation, at the Lock 3 Park along the Welland Canal in St. Catharines on August 8, 1984. Otherwise all that remains of this fine old hull are pleasant memories.

BLACK RIVER upbound on the final voyage for Q.&O.
(AS)

The ship was resold and refitted as TUXPANCLIFFE
(SG)

PIC RIVER

Pic River had preceeded Black River from the F.W. Wheeler and Company shipyard at West Bay City in 1896. The former being Hull 117 and the latter Hull 118. Both were steel consort barges.

Pic River was christened James Nasmyth and its career paralleled its running mate through six different owners prior to joining Q.&O. They always seemed to move along in tandem.

James Nasmyth was easily the more famous of the pair due to an incident off Duluth in 1905.

The ship, loaded with iron ore, cleared Duluth for the lower lakes behind the powered steamer Mataafa late in November 1905. One of the famous "gales of November" was soon to cause havoc all over the lake and Mataafa and James Nasmyth were caught.

The Master of the Mataafa decided to return to Duluth for shelter but knew the running seas would make it impossible to tow the heavily laden barge back to port.

The tow line was cut and James Nasmyth was left out on the lake.

Mataafa could not reach safety and the ship was wrecked off the mouth of the Duluth harbour. The hull cracked in three pieces and nine sailors perished of exposure in the after end.

A double tragedy was expected but when the storm finally subsided the powerless James Nasmyth was found safely anchored with its crew intact.

In 1937 James Nasmyth became the Merle H. and the Pic River in 1949.

Q.&O. operated the vessel in the pulpwood trade to Thorold and it joined Black River on drydock during the 1952 season.

The 373 foot (113.7 metre) Pic River entered service on April 11, 1953, and cleared Thorold six days later with its first cargo, newsprint, for Chicago. Eight similar loads followed that year. Pulpwood, coal and grain all out of Heron Bay, the Lakehead and Chicago brought the season total to twenty-nine payloads.

The coal was delivered to Midland, Britt and Marathon while the grain travelled to Port Colborne, Midland, Detroit and Prescott.

The careers of these two ships continued to parallel one another. Pic also averaged 26 cargoes per year. It found 1956 as the busiest season when it handled 35 payloads, one more than the Black.

Although their actual cargoes varied, both ships carried thirty different types of cargo in their Q.&O. careers. Pic did carry sand, flax, bauxite, stone and ferrous chrome while Black apparently did not.

The latter compensated by hauling fluorspar, sorghums, gluten feed pellets, slag and trucks.

Among the top ten leading ports Pic River included nine of those tallied on Black River's record although the order varied slightly. Pic rated Cleveland the tenth most common loading port stopping for salt on fifteen occasions while Black River visited but twice.

The top ten loading ports accounted for 79.8 per cent of the Pic River cargoes while the remaining thirty-eight ports for only 20.2 per cent.

The top eight discharge ports for Pic paralleled, in occasional different order, those of the sistership. Port Colborne and Midland, however, managed ninth and tenth among Pic's forty-seven unloading ports.

Like Black River, no pulpwood was carried after 1972 and newsprint was handled each season with the exception of one. In Pic's case the year without this cargo was 1975. It does appear that the port of Chicago was visited by Pic River in each of its twenty-six seasons of trading.

On September 20, 1978, Pic River cleared Baie Comeau for the last time hauling newsprint for Chicago.

The vessel then proceeded to Thunder Bay and took on 209,030 bushels of barley for Toronto. It arrived October 17.

After discharge Pic River was sold to the scrap firm of United Metals and sailed for Hamilton, Ontario. It arrived October 25 and was retired.

The tug ROCKY RIVER tows the empty barge PIC RIVER up the Welland Canal for another load of pulpwood (Q.&O. files)

During these later years Pic River made news on two occasions. On December 16, 1972, it closed navigation through the Welland Canal and proved to be the last ship to use the old, winding, channel through the City of Welland. The Welland By-Pass was opened at the start of the 1973 season and eliminated the old section.

Then, on December 7, 1977, the Pic River closed the Canadian Soo Lock for the season. It was thought at the time that the old lock would not reopen in 1978 but the guesses proved false.

Unlike Black River, there would be no reprieve for the Pic. But the ship did outlast its old running mate.

The vessel's name was officially changed to Pic R. in 1978 but the hull was untouched until 1984. Then, in March scrapping operations got underway and the valiant old vessel, after 88 years on the lakes, was gradually dismantled.

PIC RIVER sits outside Port Weller Drydocks awaiting reconstruction (W.E. Shore photo, Q.&O. files)

Her stern removed, PIC RIVER sits on the shelf at Port Weller (Q.&O. files)

PIC RIVER on Lake Ontario (AS)

ROCKY RIVER

During the late 19th Century a number of steel barges were built as successors to the old, and small, schooner barges. These consorts were about the same size as the steel steamers of the day (350 - 450 feet/100 - 140 metres long) and they were towed by these ships.

The economics were obvious. You could carry twice as much cargo with only a fifty per cent increase in crew and a slightly larger fuel bill.

These consorts served well in the iron ore trade and later carried considerable grain and other cargoes. Some consorts, such as Heron Bay, were eventually powered and by the end of the Second World War some had been scrapped.

In 1949 Q.&O. purchased two such barges along with the tug Rocky River.

These ships were used in the pulpwood trade from Lake Superior. One barge was loaded and Rocky River would tow it to Thorold for unloading before returning it north. By then the second barge would be ready for the trip to Thorold.

On occasion, during the good weather of the sum-mer, regulations allowed Rocky River to tow both barges at one time.

Rocker River was a diesel powered, wooden hulled tug. It had been built at Everett, Washington, in 1944 by the Pacific Shipbuilding and Drydock Company. The vessel was a big tug measuring 174.5 feet long (53.2 metres) and was registered at 874 gross tons.

Christened Satinleaf, the ship was originally owned by the United States Navy. But in 1947 it came to the inland seas after a sale to the Great Lakes Lumber and Shipping Company.

Q.&O. renamed the vessel Rocky River and it towed Pic River and Black River for a few years before the barges were redesigned as diesel powered carriers.

Rocky River was then sold to Foundation Maritime and moved to the Canadian East Coast as Foundation Josephine II. There it worked as salvage tug.

In 1960 this ship was resold and now became North Star IV. It sailed only briefly. On August 14, 1961, it was abandoned while aground in James Bay in Northern Canada.

BAIE COMEAU /
JOSEPH MEDILL PATTERSON

Although the reality of the long anticipated St. Lawrence Seaway project was in sight, the cargo demands of the early fifties required new tonnage capable of trading between the Great Lakes and St. Lawrence.

Q.&O. needed to add to their fleet for the newsprint and pulpwood trades. As a result they turned to a relatively new firm, the Atlantic Shipbuilding Company of Newport, Monmouthshire, England. Two vessels were ordered, hulls three and four, for delivery in 1954.

The first of the pair was launched as Baie Comeau and honoured the town created by the company in 1936. The ship was a twin screw 1,220 horsepower diesel powered freighter of 2,300 gross tons and she measured 259 feet (78.9 metres) in overall length.

Improved construction techniques permitted a carrying capacity in the range of 3,420 tons deadweight.

After her builder's trials, Baie Comeau crossed the Atlantic to work in the pulpwood and newsprint trades. She quickly proved to be a good carrier but would not retain her name for long

In 1955 it was decided to rename the two newly built ships in honour of the key participants in the parent Tribune Company. Baie Comeau thus became Joseph Medill Patterson, after the founder of the New York Daily News, after but one short season.

Newsprint and pulpwood remained the backbone of this ship's activities. When the Seaway opened in 1959 things changed a little in the early years. But gradually the larger ships garnered more of the pulpwood trade.

The Patterson hauled some grain and other bulk cargoes and this took her to ports not previously visited.

Great Lakes service continued into the 1967 season but late in the spring the vessel tied up at Port Dalhousie above Lock 1 of the Third Welland Canal.

She was idle much of the summer and late in the year sold to Shallow Draft Bulk Carriers of Bahamas. The vessel left the lakes in December under her own power and was refitted at Halifax for trading on the warmer waters of the West Indies. The ship was renamed Exuma Sound.

There are no records available of this ship's travels after leaving the lakes but it is known that for a time shipments of bauxite were carried from inland river ports in South America to transshipment centres.

Ownership is known to have moved to the Rita Shipping Company in 1972 and then, a year later, to the Caribbean Steamship Company. Under the latter firm the ship was registered in Panama. Interestingly, due to the buoyancy of saltwater, her carrying capacity was increased to 3,617 tons.

Officially the fate of Exuma Sound is unknown. Lloyds Register for 1986 lists her as "continued existence in doubt." Yet recently we have been provided with a photo, taken at Miami in 1975, of a Rita II. There is no doubt that this vessel was either Joseph Medill Patterson or Col. Robert R. McCormick. We suspect that it is the former but we have not been able to positively confirm this.

BAIE COMEAU on her trial run (Q.&O. files)

JOSEPH MEDILL PATTERSON in the Welland Canal (R.T. McCannell photo)

RITA II shown at Miami in 1976 (Emory Massman photo)

MANICOUAGAN (ii)/
COL. ROBERT R. McCORMICK

The second new vessel followed from the Atlantic Shipbuilding yard in 1955. She too carried a historic company name, that of Manicouagan, a river near Baie Comeau.

Dimensions were similar to her sistership but Manicouagan's gross tonnage was slightly greater at 2,313 tons.

After crossing the Atlantic, Manicouagan became active in the transportation of newsprint and pulpwood. After limited service in 1955 her name was changed to Col. Robert R. McCormick.

It was noted that in July 1958 this vessel was among the last to use the old canals before flooding of the Seaway prior to the opening of the U.S. locks at Massena, New York.

Col. Robert R. McCormick joined the Patterson at Port Dalhousie in early 1967. She was the first of the pair to leave and passed down the Seaway on October 4 for a refit at Halifax and new duties.

Both were owned by Shallow Draft Bulk Carriers and they renamed the McCormick, the Montagu Bay. As such she operated among the West Indies and primarily served the bauxite trade from inland river ports to transshipment centres. On one occasion, at Everton, Guyana, on the Berbice River, the vessel suffered an engine room fire. For-

tunately damage was not serious.

Montagu Bay briefly returned to Canada in 1969 but only came inland as far as Montreal before heading south once again.

The Rita Shipping Company was also listed as this ship's owner in 1972 and then the Caribbean Steamship Company a year later. Obviously she and her sistership travelled together.

Their ways parted in 1977 when Montagu Bay was sold to the All Trading Company. They renamed her Linda.

In May 1977 Linda grounded on Molasses Reef off the Florida Keys. The vessel was released and towed to Miami for unloading and inspection. Enroute she grounded once again and this time blocked the shipping channel.

The United States Coast Guard then took responsibility to move the vessel and unload her. No bond was posted and, as the condition of the vessel had deteriorated and the owners disappeared, it was decided to sink the Linda.

A final tow took her sixteen miles out to sea off the Florida Coast and on December 21, 1977, dynamite charges were set off to send the ship to the bottom.

The MANICOUAGAN looked splendid when she entered service (Q.&O. files)

COL. ROBERT R. McCORMICK has a full deckload of newsprint and ready to leave Thorold
(Al Sagon-King photo)

OUTARDE (ii)

The second Outarde was the fifth and final name carried on this freighter. It too was purchased from the Midland Steamship Company at the end of 1962 and joined Q.&O. as part of Comet Enterprises.

The Hawgood fleet, a historic lake operation at the turn of the century, had this ship built in 1906 at the Superior Shipbuilding Company yard in Superior, Wisconsin. The 545 foot (166.1 metre) freighter was christened Abraham Stearn and sailed in the ore trade. She also carried some coal and grain.

At the dissolution of the Hawgood fleet in 1914 Abraham Stearn was repossessed by the American Shipbuilding Company, heirs of the Superior yard. They chartered the vessel to Hanna's Calumet Transportation Company and it sailed as the Edward N. Saunders Jr. In 1918 another Hanna enterprise, the Producers Steamship Company, became owner.

Then, in 1931, the vessel took the name John C. Williams as part of the National Steel Corporation. This lasted until 1946 when the well travelled hull moved to the Midland Steamship Company.

Late in the first season, on November 21, 1946, John C. Williams was mauled by one of the gales of November.

For protection the ship hugged the north shore. When it arrived at Duluth it required thirty-six hours to remove tons of ice before the hatches could be opened.

During her ten year career, from 1946 to 1955, John C. Williams carried 356 cargoes. Most, 203, were ore but she also transported 86 loads of coal, 15 of grain and, on 52 occasions beginning in 1950, the vessel took deckloads of new automobiles.

Superior, at 32.6% of all cargoes, was the main loading port during this period while Duluth, recipient of coal and autos, was the chief discharge port. It accounted for

The JOHN C. WILLIAMS looked different in pre-Q.&O. years (Great Lakes Graphics)

**OUTARDE brought large loads of wood
from Baie Comeau (Robert Walton photo)**

19.2% of the payloads.

Midland renamed this ship Michael K. Tewksbury in 1956 and it spent seven years under this name.

On January 22, 1959, the Tewksbury made national news as the victim of a runaway freighter at Buffalo. The MacGilvray Shiras broke loose in high water and was swept down stream demolishing a bridge and damaging the Tewksbury and another vessel. The runaway vessel was never repaired but the other two returned to service.

On joining Q.&O. for the 1963 season Outarde concentrated in hauling pulpwood to Thorold much of the time. But in later years grain dominated the annual log. She also carried considerable quantities of salt and ore. One unusual shipment was a split load of rutile and zircon taken on at Contracoeur, Quebec, for delivery to Montreal and Ashtabula, Ohio.

Thorold, Montreal, Prescott, Toronto and Baie Comeau were the main unloading ports.

Outarde was powered by a triple expansion engine of 1,760 horsepower. This was a common power plant installed in ships built in the early part of the century. She was originally coal-fired but this was changed so that in later years she burned oil.

Outarde outlived Thorold by two years. After carrying twenty-one payloads in 1973 it took a final shipment of grain out of Thunder Bay for Prescott. She arrived at the latter port on December 6 to unload and then moved to Montreal December 8, to lay-up.

Sold to Marine Salvage for scrap, the Outarde left for overseas on April 29, 1974, under tow and was broken up.

THOROLD (iii)

With the opening of the Seaway in 1959 the Canadian shipping fleets lacked the large carriers needed to meet the new cargo transportation demands. A short term solution, adopted by most fleets, was to purchase American bulk carriers that were no longer competitive in the upper lakes ore trade. Q.&O. began to revamp their fleet in a similar way.

Two ships were acquired late in 1962 from the Midland Steamship Company and placed in a subsidiary called Comet Enterprises. Midland was shutting down operations after over thirty years on the lakes and a number of their vessels went to scrap.

The newer of this pair dated from 1917 and construction by the American Shipbuilding Company at Lorain, Ohio. It was renamed Thorold.

This vessel was 550 feet long (167.6 metres) and could carry in the range of 11,000 tons deadweight or 400,000 bushels of grain. It was powered by a triple expansion engine.

The ship had been ordered before the United States entered World War One and it was requisitioned while under construction. The vessel was eventually released by the U.S. Shipping Board to aid in the transportation of ore. The Producers Steamship Company sent it to work as Carmi A. Thompson.

The ship later served the National Steel Corporation and the Butler Steamship Company before joining the Midland fleet.

This was first and foremost an ore carrier and it ran from the docks of Lake Superior to the lower lakes. During a five year period, from mid-1942 to mid-1947, this vessel hauled 145 cargoes. Eighty per cent were ore, 16.5% coal and 3.5% grain.

Superior was easily the most popular loading port as Carmi A. Thompson called there 81 times. Two Harbors, Minnesota, was next with 23 stops while Duluth, Sandusky and Toledo followed.

Ore cargoes to Ashtabula and Indiana Harbor dominated with 48 moving to the former port and 44 to the latter. A total of fifteen cities were visited including single stops at Sault Ste. Marie, Ontario, and Fort William.

Moving pulpwood from the Gulf of St. Lawrence to her namesake port was the main task for Thorold on joining the Q.&O. fleet.

Standard bulk carriers, such as Thorold, had previously hauled pulpwood on deck in neat stacks. In the late sixties this was changed after a successful experiment with the Thorold.

While loading at Baie Comeau, only one tier of wood was piled around the perimeter of Thorold's deck. The rest of the cargo was then dumped inside the piles. This method proved successful and was an obvious time and labour saver. As a result the new system, which had been in use in specialized pulp carriers, became the standard means of loading deck cargoes of pulpwood for all Q.&O. ships.

CARMI A. THOMPSON was an ore carrier before joining the fleet (Emory Massman photo)

As THOROLD she brought many loads of pulpwood from the St. Lawrence (Q.&O. files)

THORO is shown at Ramey's Bend
on July 25, 1972 (SG)

As a backhaul down the St. Lawrence Thorold carried grain with Montreal, Prescott, and Baie Comeau the most popular stops.

Occasionally this vessel brought ore from the ranges of Quebec, loading mainly at Pointe Noire, to American destinations. She also carried salt, coal, coke and sugar beet pellets plus several shipments of newsprint.

Her last cargo, 438,233.9 bushels of grain, cleared the Lakeshead December 6, 1971. After discharging at Prescott, Thorold sailed for Port Colborne and arrived at the Ramey's Bend scrapyard of Marine Salvage on December 18.

The vessel's name was shortened to Thoro in 1972 to release the historic company name for the fourth such ship in the fleet. During that year the men of Marine Salvage gradually dismantled the hull.

One of Thorold's two sisterships survives as the popular tourist attraction and museum ship Valley Camp at Sault Ste. Marie, Michigan.

SHELTER BAY (ii)

With Thorold and Outarde successfully established in the Q.&O. service, the company sought a third vessel for the expanding Seaway trades.

They turned to the Interlake Steamship Company and completed a deal to purchase their idle Jay C. Morse. The vessel had been laid up at South Chicago since 1960 and the prospects of a return to work in that fleet were gone.

When this ship had been built at Cleveland in 1907 it was the largest member of the Pickands-Mather fleet. It also became, temporarily, the largest in the Q.&O. fleet as its length of 552 feet (168.4 metres) exceeded previous acquisitions.

Christened Jay C. Morse, this vessel plied the upper lakes hauling bulk cargoes for almost sixty years. Her service was generally uneventful but it is noted that she received a new pilothouse during the winter of 1953—54.

During the 1956 season the Morse hauled 32 payloads. Ore was the leader with 22 cargoes. In addition there were nine shipments of coal and one of stone. Jay C. Morse was laid up at Mukdegon, Michigan, from July 8 to August 1 due to a lack of work.

On April 9, 1965, this vessel cleared South Chicago for Q.&O. It encountered heavy ice in the Straits of Machinac but reached Port Colborne April 11 to be refitted as Shelter Bay.

That season the ship totalled 21 cargoes and nine of these were iron ore. All loaded at Pointe Noire, Quebec, and were delivered to South Chicago, Indiana Harbor, Toledo and Cleveland.

She carried eight shipments of grain, mostly from South Chicago to Baie Comeau.

Two cargoes of salt out of Cleveland and Detroit went to Montreal and Quebec City while a single load of coal travelled from South Chicago to Marathon, Ontario. Her one trip with newsprint originated at Baie Comeau with Chicago as destination.

Although no pulpwood was carried that first year with Q.&O. the vessel soon swung into that trade between Baie Comeau and Thorold. Shelter Bay also carried considerable grain, mainly out of Thunder Bay, salt from Ojibway, ore from Pointe Noire and coal out of Toledo.

One unusual trip in 1973 saw Shelter Bay carry a load of towers totalling 146 tons. These loaded at Lauzon, Quebec, for Port Cartier, Quebec.

Like many other company ships, Toronto was the main discharge port, especially in the last decade of service. Trips to Thorold, however, ceased after 1974.

Q.&O. had the vessel rebuilt in 1966 with a pair of used Scotch boilers from the retired laker Bayton. Early in 1967, on May 2, Shelter Bay grounded in the Brockville Narrows and holed. She was released May 4 and, after unloading, had to go to Port Weller Drydocks for repairs.

Shelter Bay also made news on April 3, 1976, when it opened the port of Toronto for the season.

Shelter Bay loaded 398,812 bushels of wheat, soybeans and barley as a last cargo and cleared Thunder Bay December 18, 1978, for Goderich, Ontario.

The vessel was sold to the Goderich Elevator Company for use as a storage barge to augment the port's elevator facilities. The ship was renamed Shelter B. in 1979 and then D.B. Weldon before the end of that year.

On May 27, 1981, the pilothouse was removed from the ship at Goderich and placed on a cement pad for use as a marine museum.

The hull continued to be used until 1983 but was then sold to Western Metals for scrap. The tug W.J. Ivan Purcis provided power for the final trip and the old Shelter Bay was towed into Thunder Bay June 11, 1983. The ship was broken up over the next year.

JAY C. MORSE served the Interlake Steamship Company for many years (Great Lakes Graphics)

SHELTER BAY handled a variety of cargoes (Tom Graham photo, courtesy Barry Andersen)

J. PIERPONT MORGAN was the first 600 footer on the lakes (Sykes collection)

HERON BAY (ii)

As the 1965 season ended Q.&O. made another addition to the fleet. This time they negotiated the purchase of the United States Steel freighter J. Pierpont Morgan.

This vessel had been idle at Duluth since November 11, 1960, but in December 1965 it moved to Port Arthur for reconditioning.

J. Pierpont Morgan was a historic ship. It had been built by the Chicago Shipbuilding Company at Chicago in 1906 and was the largest vessel on the Great Lakes in an era still dominated by schooners and wooden steamers.

The vessel was the first on the lakes to reach 600 feet (182.8 metres) overall length measuring 601 feet long. This giant vessel concentrated in the ore trade for the Pittsburgh Steamship Division of U.S Steel hauling payloads of around 12,000 tons at a time. She usually loaded at the iron range docks around Lake Superior for company docks down the lakes.

The Morgan served the company well through two World Wars but as newer vessels were built and ore demand lessened the ship was sent to the wall.

However, Q.&O., through their Comet Enterprises subsidiary, offered a new lease on life. This bulk freighter began the 1966 season as Heron Bay.

The vessel did not prove to be as good a carrier for pulpwood as the other recent acquisitions but Heron Bay carried the cargo on occasion.

Transportation of ore and wheat were the major sources of work for Heron Bay. But she also carried considerable salt.

Thunder Bay, Ojibway and Toledo were the main loading ports as well as the St. Lawrence centres of Sept Iles and Pointe Noire.

Montreal and Toronto, recipients of both grain and salt, were the major discharge ports. Towards the end of her service the ship also made frequent stops at Contracoeur, Quebec, with coke from Cleveland and Buffalo.

As Heron Bay did not have as many cargoes running from Thunder Bay down the full length of the Seaway she was able to get in more trips per year than some of the other company ships. Her peak year appears to be 1970 when the ship carried 34 cargoes and included stops at twenty different communities.

Heron Bay loaded a final cargo of 424,000 bushels of wheat at Duluth and passed down the Welland Canal for the last time on October 20, 1978. After unloading at Port Cartier the vessel proceeded to Lauzon, Quebec, and laid up November 4.

The ship's name was shortened to Heron B. Then, on March 30, 1979, work on breaking up the hull for scrap got underway and was apparently completed later in the year.

HERON BAY at Sault Ste. Marie on June 20, 1977 (Rev. Peter VanderLinden, photo)

FRANQUELIN (ii)

In 1967 Q.&O. purchased two small bulk carriers from Mohawk Navigation. They were good acquisitions and the vessels served the company until its demise.

Franquelin, the older of the pair, was built in St. Catharines, Ontario, by Port Weller Drydocks. The vessel was their Hull 18 and was launched in 1955 as Griffon.

The ship joined the Beaconsfield Steamship Company and, as she had dimensions suitable for trading through the old St. Lawrence Canals, worked much of the time in the river trade.

The opening of the Seaway ended the competitive advantage of the smaller ships so Griffon was lengthened from 259 feet (78.9 metres) overall to 343 feet (104.5 metres). This was done in two stages by Canadian Vickers at Montreal in 1959 and 1960. The vessel was also deepened. Accordingly the ship could carry close to 6,000 tons per trip with the new dimensions.

Ownership was transferred to Mohawk Navigation in 1963 and the ship earned her keep around the Seaway in their colours until the sale to Q.&O. in 1967.

Renamed Franquelin, this ship was engaged in many trades. Newsprint from Thorold to Chicago dominated the early years but the ship handled considerable grain as well. Barley, wheat, corn, soybeans, malt, oats, rye and flax were all loaded aboard Franquelin at one time or another. Often two or more grains were carried, in separate holds, at the same time. Various grain cargoes accounted for 52% of all payloads.

As newsprint cargoes declined other commodities were found as replacements to keep this versatile ship busy. The vessel carried salt, mostly out of Pugwash, Nova Scotia, with lesser amounts from Windsor, Ojibway, Goderich, Detroit and Fairport.

Franquelin also hauled eighteen loads of pitch from Detroit to Baie Comeau and ten cargoes of zinc concentrates. The latter loaded at Hawke Bay, Newfoundland, and most went to Valleyfield, Quebec.

Other cargoes transported by Franquelin included clay, pig iron, coke, steel, grinding balls, sand, phosphate, bauxite, sugar, calcium chloride and a load of incinerator ash.

GRIFFON was built with canal-sized dimensions and is shown at Cleveland in 1957 (Pete Worden photo)

As could be expected, Thunder Bay led the thirty-five loading ports served by this ship. Thorold dominated the early years but the vessel did not load there after taking out eleven cargoes of newsprint in 1972.

More of this ship's cargoes went to Toronto than anywhere else. Those were usually grain. Chicago, Prescott, Montreal, Baie Comeau, Chicoutimi, Goderich and Duluth ranked next in the list of popular unloading ports.

Among the ports visited on a limited basis for Franquelin were Muskegon, Michigan; Manitowoc, Wisconsin; Cleveland, Ohio; Marathon and Cardinal, Ontario. All told she called on at least forty different places to discharge.

The vessel's busiest year for Q.&O. was twenty-seven cargoes and these were carried in each of 1970, 1973, 1975 and 1977.

Occasionally this 1,800 horsepower diesel powered vessel was delayed by minor accidents. On December 19, 1976, an early arrival of ice caused problems and the ship grounded for seven hours off Algonac, Michigan. A day later ice forced Franquelin out of the channel in Lake St. Clair.

In another incident, on September 26, 1978, this ship went on below Beauharnois, Quebec. After refloating, it went to Montreal for repairs and was caught at the drydock due to a strike.

The small size of Franquelin has proven to be useful in this era of the thousand footer. On November 15, 1979, the ship wound its way upriver to Wallaceburg, Ontario, to load corn. It was the largest ship to that port in years and it has returned on a number of occasions.

Even in its last year for Q.&O. Franquelin made headlines. On April 23, 1983, the ship opened the season at Collingwood, Ont., unloading mixed feed grain. Two days later the ship opened the neighbouring port of Owen Sound loading wheat.

Desgagnes acquired Franquelin and has kept it busy. As the 1987 season began this vessel re-entered service as Eva Desgagnes. It continues to trade throughout the lakes. Grain, pitch, salt, coal, pig iron and clay are still loaded aboard as they were in the Q.&O. days.

FRANQUELIN was upbound in Lock 4 on October 31, 1981 (SG)

NEW YORK NEWS (iii)

New York News is a sistership to Franquelin and followed her at the Port Weller Drydocks yard as Hull 19. She went into service in 1956 for Beaconsfield Steamships as Tecumseh.

The iron ore ranges of Quebec and Labrador opened in the mid-fifties but the construction of the Seaway was not complete. This kept the larger vessels from coming in and out of the Great Lakes system.

In July 1958 Tecumseh was the last vessel upbound through the old Cornwall Canal before that area was flooded and replaced by the modern Seaway locks.

Tecumseh and her sister Griffon, were examples of modern canal-sized ships that were designed to carry a greater payload than their predecessors in the canal trade. They were initial successes but once the Seaway commenced in 1959 they needed to find new work.

Like her sistership, Tecumseh was deepened and lengthened by Canadian Vickers at Montreal in 1959—60. The vessel emerged as 343 feet long by 44 feet at the beam (104.5 x 13.4 metres). Tonnage was registered at 3,436 gross and her carrying capacity was 5,900 tons deadweight.

A transfer, in 1963, brought Tecumseh into Mohawk Navigation colours and then a sale in 1967 sent the ship to Q.&O. The latter renamed her New York News.

The early days in company colours were not the best. On July 9 the ship was in collision with the Nordglimt off Escoumins. Damage was light.

It was much more serious July 18 when the vessel buckled and sank while loading salt at Pugwash, Nova Scotia. The ship had to be salvaged in two parts and towed

TECUMSEH was lengthened prior to joining Q.&O.
(Robert Walton photo)

An accident at Pugwash, N.S., left NEW YORK NEWS in two pieces (Rev. Carl Hall photo)

to Halifax, Nova Scotia, for repairs. There the ship was drydocked and rejoined.

From 1968 on New York News cargoes were similar to those of Franquelin. But she did carry a little more wheat, corn, clay, zinc, pig iron and barley malt than her sister.

She also handled limited amounts of pulpwood, slag and gravel which had not been carried by her sister.

Thunder Bay, Thorold, Baie Comeau, Detroit and Windsor were the five most popular loading ports for New York News. These accounted for 58.8% of all cargoes. There were 32 different loading ports and also included single visits to Huron, Ohio, Saginaw, Michigan, and Clarke City, Quebec. Pelee Island, Port Stanley and Wallaceburg, all in Ontario, were common stops toward the end of the ship's travels with Q.&O.

Toronto, Chicago, Duluth, Baie Comeau and Goderich were the main ports where New York News unloaded. All told both ships called at forty different discharge ports each.

On two occasions, 1980 and 1981, New York News carried 28 cargoes for the year. These were the highest totals during her stint in the fleet.

Two minor groundings were the only incidents in later years. In one, September 18, 1979, the vessel grounded off the mouth of the Detroit River. Then, on August 11, 1982, it spent time on a sandbar off Ogdensburg, N.Y. Tugs came to her aid in both instances.

New York News joined the Desgagnes fleet for the 1984 season. She was renamed Stella Desgagnes in 1986 and opened navigation at Wallaceburg that year on June 11.

New York News and Franquelin have outlived most of the other pre-Seaway St. Lawrence canal vessels. One hopes that these former members of the Q.&O. fleet will be around for many more years.

STELLA DESGAGNES continues as part of the Desgagnes fleet (SG)

NEW YORK NEWS and FRANQUELIN often wintered at Toronto and are shown on January 23, 1971 (SG)

THOROLD (iv)

The fourth ship to sail as Thorold had originally been a deep sea bulk carrier. It was built by Hall, Russell & Co. at Aberdeen, Scotland, in 1962 for the Burnett Steamship Company.

Christened Gosforth, it began visiting the Seaway immediately and by the end of 1967 had made twenty-one transits in and out of the lakes.

Q.&O. purchased the ship in 1972 through the Trico Enterprises subsidiary. The vessel was refitted at Sorel to carry newsprint on the lakes and Atlantic. On the final day of July it entered service clearing Baie Comeau with 4,786 tons of newsprint for the Florida ports of Port Canaveral and Port Everglades.

In the seasons that followed Thorold hauled 235 cargoes. Newsprint accounted for 37% of all shipments while mixed grain and wheat totalled 34.9%.

Thorold loaded at Baie Comeau for 36.6% of the time and Thunder Bay for 35.9%. Unusual loading ports included Baie Verte, Cornerbrook and Fisher Harbor, Newfoundland, Beaumont, Texas, Gravesend, England, and Rouen, France.

Halifax received 22.1% of all cargoes, mostly grain, while Chicago was the unloading port for 15.7% of all loads. Most of the latter were newsprint.

Deep sea stops also included Alexandria and Richmond, Virginia, Jacksonville, Florida, Houston, Texas, plus Liverpool and London, England. On December 14, 1976, Thorold took an unusual shipment of 424 tons of submarine parts out of Montreal for Quincy, Massachusetts.

This versatile carrier also handled considerable amounts of zinc, salt, phosphates, pig iron and gypsum plus single loads of sulphur, grinding balls, calcium chloride and quartzite.

During one stretch in 1974 Thorold was chartered to Algoma Steel to haul seven loads of steel ingots from Sault Ste. Marie, Ontario, to Burns Harbor, Indiana, and return with coiled steel.

Thorold brought 5,372 metric tonnes of malt into Toronto in December 1983 as her final Q.&O. cargo. She resumed trading in 1984 for Desgagnes and has continued service on the Great Lakes and St. Lawrence Seaway.

Since 1985 this vessel has operated as Catharine Desgagnes. She still sees some deep sea work and travelled to the Arctic in 1984 on the resupply run to northern ports. Then, in May 1987, it had a trip to the U.S. Gulf coast with pig iron.

Navigation on the shallow lakes and rivers of the Seaway is not an easy task and groundings often occur. Thorold has not been spared these problems.

On November 22, 1974, this 410 foot (125 metre) carrier went aground at Goderich. Later, on August 21, 1981, and April 22, 1983, it grounded on the St. Lawrence. On both occasions the ship was bound for Halifax with grain.

Finally, on January 13, 1985, the vessel grounded on Red Islet near the mouth of the Saguenay River while carrying salt from the Magdalen Islands to Montreal.

The diesel powered Thorold proved to be not only a good carrier in the vital newsprint trade for Q.&O. but served the company and a later owner as a valued general purpose vessel.

GOSFORTH was originally a deep sea freighter (Courtesy George Corbin)

When THOROLD had to drop anchor in the Welland Canal, divers were called to be sure it had not snagged a main or cable (Denis Cahill, St. Catharines Standard)

GOLDEN HIND

Golden Hind sailed for eleven years in the Q.&O. fleet and carried a total of 258 cargoes.

Wheat accounted for 45.5% of the shipments while ore followed at 22.9% and barley at 10.3%. There were fifteen different commodities handled including single loads of bentonite, sand, fluorspar and pig iron. All were unusual for a straight deck bulk carrier of this size.

Thunder Bay was easily the most popular loading port accounting for 53.1% of all cargoes. Sept-Iles, at 15.5%, followed among the twenty-one loading ports.

Baie Comeau and Montreal, at 12.6% and 11.8% respectively, led the twenty-eight discharge ports. Sorel, Prescott and Quebec City all received about 10% of the vessel's shipments.

Golden Hind joined the Q.&O. fleet in 1973 and was the first and only steam turbine driven ship in the company. During that year the ship travelled 49,360 miles. It ran loaded 44.5% of the time, light 20.3% of the time and spent 17.6% of the time at a discharge port and 17.5% at a loading port.

Actual loading and unloading time were only four and five per cent respectively. The rest of the port time included the inevitable delays.

This vessel was designed to carry petroleum and was the third of three sisterships built by Imperial Oil. All were engaged in hauling crude oil from Superior, Wisconsin, to Sarnia, Ontario.

She was to serve only two seasons on this route. The vessel had been launched at Collingwood December 6, 1951, and entered service the following April 12.

By the end of the 1953 season a pipeline had been extended to Sarnia and the ships were no longer needed to bring the newly discovered Western Canadian crude to the refinery.

Mohawk Navigation purchased this ship and it was rebuilt at Humberstone, Ontario as a bulk carier. The 620 foot (189 metre) carrier was reregistered at 12,304 gross tons and had a carrying capacity of 16,700 tons deadweight.

Renamed Golden Hind, this vessel was the largest

IMPERIAL WOODBEND was a tanker on June 19, 1953 (J.H. Bascom photo)

GOLDEN HIND, in Mohawk Navigation colours, off Port Weller on October 3, 1971 (SG)

member of the Mohawk fleet. In the early, pre-Seaway years, it traded into the Georgian Bay ports and east to Prescott with grain. Starting in 1959 it travelled to the Gulf of St. Lawrence and often brought iron ore back to the lakes.

Scott Misener Steamships chartered Golden Hind from 1969 through the 1972 season. It was then purchased by Q.&O.

On three occasions Golden Hind went aground. On May 15, 1967, the vessel got caught on a reef on Lake Erie and was holed in the forward compartment.

Then, on June 18, 1979, it grounded on the St. Lawrence off Port Neuf, Quebec, and required six weeks at Port Weller Drydocks to return to ship to work.

Finally, on August 12, 1982, the vessel found the bottom at Sault Ste. Marie. Fortunately this accident was not as severe.

Golden Hind brought her final Q.&O. cargo to Toronto on December 18, 1983. It was 13,372 metric tonnes of malt barley and this was unloaded during the winter.

In the final year with the company this ship made 24 trips. Almost all was with grain and totalled 349,037 metric tonnes.

Golden Hind joined Desgagnes Transports but only saw a few weeks of work late in the 1985 season. It laid up at Toronto for the last time on December 29.

The only trip that remained cleared September 9, 1986, for the St. Lawrence. The vessel left Quebec City September 29 behind the Polish tug Koral bound for Columbia.

Golden Hind arrived at the port of Mamonal with another retired Canadian freighter, John E.F. Misener, on October 28. Both ships were cut up for scrap.

GOLDEN HIND was operating for Q.&O. on October 27, 1973 (SG)

OUTARDE (iii)

The third ship to carry the Outarde name in Q.&O. colours was one of four sisterships. Each had been built for the Interlake Steamship Company in the mid-twenties and three eventually found their way to Canadian registry.

Outarde was originally the Robert Hobson. It was built by the American Steamship Company at Lorain, Ohio, in 1927 and measured 600 feet long by 60 feet at the beam (182 × 18.2 metres). Vessels of similar size and capacity were common in the U.S. Great Lakes fleet and they served as the backbone of the ore trade for almost half a century.

Robert Hobson was named for a Canadian who had been President of the Steel Company of Canada from 1916 until his death in 1926. The vessel operated under this name and the Interlake banner until part way into the 1975 season. At that time it was laid up at Ashtabula, Ohio.

Marine Salvage of Port Colborne purchased the ship for scrap and towed the vessel to their yard. It arrived August 9, 1975. Within a month the ship had been resold to Q.&O. for service under Canadian registry.

Renamed Outarde (C348593), it re-entered service September 26 headed for Walkerville, Ontario. There it took on grain for discharge at Port McNicoll, Ontario.

Outarde spent nine seasons in the Q.&O. fleet and was a fine addition. It carried 196 cargoes in those years with wheat, which accounted for 29.6% of the payloads, being dominant. Ore, at 28.1%, was a close second while grain, corn and coke accounted for an additional 28.1%. Lesser amounts of pig iron, barley, soybeans, sand/slag, salt, barley/malt, sugar, sand and bauxite completing the cargo list.

Thunder Bay, with 44.4% of the cargoes, was the chief loading port. Interestingly, the small Lake Erie community of Port Stanley, ranked second. Outarde visited thirty different ports around the Great Lakes to take on cargo.

Indiana Harbor on Lake Michigan received 18.4%

of Outarde's cargoes but most of these occurred in 1978 and 1979. In those years the vessel hauled ore out of Thunder Bay to that port for Inland Steel.

The grain receiving centres of Prescott, Montreal, Sorel and Quebec City were the next most popular among the thirty-two discharge ports visited by the ship.

Outarde took on her last cargo, a shipment of 11,003 metric tonnes of barley at Thunder Bay on December 15, 1983. When the ship tied up at Toronto December 21 her sailing career had ended.

Desgagnes was able to put the smaller Q.&O. acquisitions back to work but Outarde remained idle at Toronto until 1985.

She was sold for scrap and towed into Port Colborne August 16, 1985, with the tugs James E. McGrath and B.J. Murer handling the last trip. The men of International Marine Salvage did not take long to dismantle the hull and by November 23 the work had been completed.

During this vessel's career a 2,300 horsepower triple expansion engine with cylinders of 24 1/2", 41", 65" and a 42" stroke supplied power. The three water tube boilers were originally coal-fired but Q.&O. had the ship converted to burn oil after the 1975 season.

There were at least four accidents involving this vessel. In 1951 it was in collision with the Lackawanna on the St. Mary's River. Then, in May 1972, it lost power at Port Huron and hit a breakwall doing a reported $100,000 in damage.

From May 8—16, 1977, Outarde was aground on the St. Lawrence near Buoy 41. Only minor damage resulted.

Finally, the ship found a mud bank off Cardinal, Ontario, in May 1983 and again there was no damage of consequence.

Thanks to the investment of Q.&O., Outarde had a ten year reprieve from scrapping and proved to be a good carrier in the company fleet.

ROBERT HOBSON had already been sold for scrap when rescued by Q.&O. (Great Lakes Graphics)

OUTARDE carried 196 cargoes for Q.&O. (AS)

OUTARDE arriving Port Weller under tow for scrap (Bill Bruce)

BAIE COMEAU II

Q.&O. needed a deep sea ship for the coastal trade in the mid-seventies and selected a Spanish vessel named Monte Almanzor. This general cargo carrier had been trading on the Mediterranean between Spain and Africa.

This was a relatively new ship having been built by Juliana Constructor Gijonesa in 1973 at Gijon, Spain. It stretched 387.5 feet (118.1 metres) in overall length and was registered at 5,306 gross tons and 3,033 net. A 4,600 brake horsepower Burmeister & Wain diesel engine provided power.

Naviera Aznar Sociedad Anonima operated this vessel. It had accommodations for 32 crew and was air conditioned.

Monte Almanzor was purchased for in excess of $3 million and arrived at Port Colborne May 20, 1977, for a refit prior to sailing for Q.&O. Work proceeded smoothly and the vessel was christened Baie Comeau II June 8 and began service on June 19.

During her six seasons in company colours Baie Comeau II carried 75 cargoes. Most, 64 or 85.3%, were newsprint. These travelled along the Atlantic coast to Port Everglades, Port Canaveral and Jacksonville, Florida, Alexandria, Va., Washington, D.C. and New York City, plus Chicago, Milwaukee and Green Bay on the Great Lakes. In addition the ship also crossed the Atlantic to discharge newsprint at Grangemouth, U.K. and Rouen, France.

The next most popular cargo for Baie Comeau II was steel. One load travelled from Montreal to Chicago in 1978 while three shipments came aboard in 1979. The latter occurred under charter to Algoma Steel at Sault Ste. Marie, Ont. to move the cargoes to Detroit and Windsor.

Mixed grain, zinc and wheat completed Baie Comeau II's Q.&O. ledger. Only nine of her total cargoes were loaded on the Great Lakes.

On January 9, 1983, this ship laid up at Sorel, Que. She was sold to a Panamanian firm, Progress Shipping, later in the year. They renamed her Agia Trias and the ship cleared for the Gulf of Mexico on October 11. There the vessel was slated to haul grain from New Orleans to ports in Mexico and around the Caribbean.

MONTE ALMANZOR had Spanish registry before joining Q.&O. (SG)

BAIE COMEAU II saw little service on the Great Lakes (AS)

AGIA TRIAS was renamed at Sorel before heading south (Rene Beauchamp photo)

BLANCHE HINDMAN / LAC STE. ANNE

Five ships were purchased from the Hindman Transportation Company after the 1977 navigation season.

The Hindman name had been active in Great Lakes trading since the early 1920's. It had been associated with several shipping companies and culminated with the formation of the Hindman Transportation Company in 1954. The sale to Q.&O. thus removed this fleet from Great Lakes registers.

Blanche Hindman had been the final addition to the Hindman fleet. Like most of their ships over the years it had been built for American interests before finally finding its way into Canadian registry.

The vessel had been built by the Great Lakes Engineering Works at Ecorse, Michigan, in 1924. It measured 612 feet long (186.5 metres), 62 feet (18.9 metres) at the beam and 32 feet (9.75 metres) in depth. Originally tonnage was registered at 8,318 gross and 6,517 net. A 2,300 horsepower triple expansion engine provided power while three coal-fired scotch boilers produced the steam requirements.

Christened Edward J. Berwind, this vessel went to work for the Franklin Steamship Company. It was managed by H.K. Oakes to 1930, Bethlehem Steel to 1941 and then M.A. Hanna. In 1943 Hanna Mining assumed ownership and the vessel served their interests for another 31 years.

During these years the Berwind concentrated on ore transportation with some cargoes of coal. On June 11, 1936, it was in collision off Long Point on Lake Erie with the small Canadian vessel Aycliffe Hall. The latter sank and resisted later efforts at salvage.

Hanna renamed the Berwind as Matthew Andrews in 1963. It was the third ship to carry this name. In 1970-71 Hanna had the ship converted to burn oil rather than coal with the work being done at Superior, Wisconsin.

Four pleasure boaters were mighty joyful to spot the Andrews on August 19, 1973. They were drifting in the dark on Green Bay, Lake Michigan, when spotted by an alert crewman. Rescue had finally arrived.

At the end of the 1973 season this ship laid up and remained idle until her sale to Hindman in October 1974. After a refit at Windsor, this vessel resumed trading as Blanche Hindman.

This was the third vessel of this name in Great Lakes

EDWARD J. BERWIND is seen on the Detroit River (Great Lakes Graphics)

service. All honoured the wife of Hindman's founder, Captain George Hindman.

Hindman kept this ship busy in a variety of trades. It operated routinely save for a grounding accident on the St. Clair River on June 3, 1977. The freighter was lightered and released June 7.

When this ship moved to Q.&O. in 1978 it had only five more years of trading left. Q.&O. retained the Hindman name for one season and then renamed her Lac Ste. Anne.

This name came from a lake north of Baie Comeau, Quebec. There the parent company owned timberlands that provided pulpwood for the newsprint mill.

During the Q.&O. years this vessel carried 99 payloads. Most, 39.9% were wheat while 25.8% were mixed grain. The vessel also hauled coke, sand, pig iron, potash, steel and bauxite as well as 15 shipments of iron ore.

The most popular of the loading ports was Thunder Bay where 57.5% of the cargoes came aboard while Sarnia was a distant second with 6.6%. Montreal received 17.1% of the shipments with Prescott, Quebec City and Sorel close behind among the 25 discharge ports.

The company had Lac Ste. Anne reboilered at Port Colborne after the 1981 season receiving a second hand set from the old Brookdale. Unfortunately the decline in shipping was not predicted and the vessel sailed only one more year.

The last cargo for Lac Ste. Anne was 11,505 metric tonnes of wheat to Prescott and it was unloaded in December 1982. The ship then moved to Hamilton to lay-up. She did not fit out in 1983 and then proceeded to Desgagnes Transports when that firm purchased the fleet.

There was no future service in sight so Desgagnes sold this vessel for scrap and it cleared April 2, 1985, under tow for Port Colborne. She laid up along the old canal bank before moving to the scrap berth above the Lock 8 on November 23, 1985.

There the men of International Marine Salvage reduced the vessel to scrap early in 1986.

BLANCHE HINDMAN served Hindman Transportation until their sale to Q.&O. (AS)

LAC STE. ANNE pushed aside ice leaving Port Colborne on April 21, 1979 (Barry Andersen photo)

LAC STE. ANNE awaits scrapping (SG)

GEORGE HINDMAN / MELDRUM BAY

There have been four ships named George Hindman in Great Lakes history. Each has honoured Captain George Hindman who was active in lakes shipping for many years and founder of the Hindman Transportation Company.

The fourth vessel of this name was the newest and largest ship in their fleet and, on joining Q. & O. proved to be the largest carrier ever in this company's history.

Indeed, when launched this vessel shared, with her sistership Hochelaga, the status of largest bulk carrier in the Canadian lake's fleet.

With World War Two concluded, American and Canadian shipowners began to renew their fleets. The first Canadian bulker to enter service after the war was Hochelaga. It was launched on August 4, 1949. This was followed by the Coverdale.

The latter was built at Midland, Ont., and measured 640 feet long by 67 feet at the beam (195.1 × 20.4 metres). Tonnage was registered at 11, 996 gross and 8,267 net.

Coverdale joined the Canada Steamship Lines fleet, Canada's largest, and set a number of Great Lakes cargo records. These included a shipment of 612,000 bushels of wheat and 17,200 tons of ore in 1950. Then, on June 5, 1951, it loaded 20,061 tons of soft coal at Ashtabula for delivery to Hamilton.

Usually this vessel carried coal to Sault Ste. Marie and ore to Hamilton. In these years Coverdale would average about 35 trips and even after 1959 rarely went down the St. Lawrence Seaway.

By 1973 this vessel had become the smallest bulker in CSL colours and it was sold to Hindman. There it once again assumed the status as largest. They renamed the ship George Hindman.

Joining Q. & O. in 1978, this ship operated another year as George Hindman before being renamed Meldrum Bay prior to the start of shipping in 1979. This honoured a once major pulpwood port on Manitoulin Island.

Meldrum Bay spent six years carrying cargoes for Q. & O. customers. There were a total of 115 different payloads.

Wheat was carried 68.7% of the time and ore accounted for 18.3% of the cargoes. The remaining payloads consisted of barley, coke, corn, soybeans and mixed grain.

The ship called at Thunder Bay to load 70.4% of the time while the Quebec Gulf ore ports of Sept Iles and Port Cartier followed at 6.1% each.

Montreal received 20.8% of this ship's payloads with Sorel, Quebec City, Trois Rivieres and Midland, all grain centres, trailing. Cleveland, followed by Conneaut and Detroit, were the most popular ports receiving shipments of ore.

Meldrum Bay took on her last cargo at Sarnia on December 18, 1983. This may have been the final load taken aboard a Q. & O. vessel and the ship arrived at Toronto on December 20 and laid up.

This ship was part of the sale to Desgagnes Navigation in 1984 but was sold for scrap the following year.

Meldrum Bay cleared Toronto July 24, 1986, with four tugs, Stormont, Glenside, Glenevis and Argue Martin, assisting in the tow down the Seaway.

After wintering at Lauzon, Quebec, the Polish tug Jantar picked up the ship in June 1987 with Lisbon, Portugal, the destination.

COVERDALE was the largest ship in three different fleets (Robert Walton photo)

GEORGE HINDMAN was renamed after a year in company colours (AS)

MELDRUM BAY is shown heading upbound above Lock 2 of the Welland Canal on August 2, 1983 (SG)

MARTHA HINDMAN / LAC DES ILES

The L.C. Smith Transportation Company ordered the construction of Hull 159 by the Detroit Shipbuilding Company of Wyandotte, Mich. This vessel was completed in 1905 and went to work as the Lyman C. Smith.

Measuring 550 feet (167.6 metres) in overall length, this was considered a large freighter in the first decades of the 20th century.

The Great Lakes Steamship Company was organized in 1911 bringing together several smaller concerns. The Lyman C. Smith acquired their colours at this time and remained in this fleet throughout its existence.

On the dissolution of the Great Lakes SS Co. in 1957 the Lyman C. Smith joined the Wilson Marine Transit Company. It remained with this firm, maintaining the original name until 1966.

No longer among the lake giants by the mid-sixties, this aging but still sound vessel could not compete in the upper lakes ore trades.

On the other hand the Canadian lakes fleet could offer several years of profitable service and, like a number of similar vessels, this ship was sold for Seaway trading.

Hindman Transportation of Owen Sound, Ontario, purchased this vessel and renamed it Martha Hindman in 1966. As such it honoured the mother of Captain George Hindman the company's founder.

Martha Hindman was registered at 7,269 gross tons, 4,604 net and had a carrying capacity of 11,200 tons of cargo. When transporting grain this amounted to 375,000 bushels.

Martha Hindman sailed for twelve years in this fleet and travelled between Lake Superior and the Gulf of St. Lawrence. The service was generally routine and free of accidents.

An exception was a galley fire while wintering at Toronto on December 31, 1974. Quick action prevented major damage and the estimated repair bill was $5,000.

The Quebec and Ontario Transportation Company put Martha Hindman to work for the 1978 season and it carried 20 cargoes on their account calling on eighteen different ports.

The last trip of the season almost ended in disaster. Entering the port of Goderich with a winter storage cargo, the ship struck the pier and tore open the hull on the starboard forward side. The ship made the dock but settled. It had to be patched, pumped out and and unloaded before permanent repairs could be completed.

The next season, 1979, saw this ship back to work as Lac Des Iles. This name recognized a lake north of Baie Comeau.

During the final two seasons this ship carried 23 and 21 cargoes respectively. This made a total of 67 shipments during the Q. & O. years. These consisted of corn — 16, wheat — 14, coke — 14, ore — 7, pig iron — 4, mixed grain — 4, soybeans — 4, barley — 2, plus single loads of rutile sand and flax. There were fifteen different loading ports and 24 different discharge centres.

On October 6, 1980, the vessel grounded below Grassy Island on the Detroit River. Lac Des Iles continued a few more weeks and, after unloading 8,779 metric tonnes of corn from Port Stanley at the elevator in Trois Rivieres, Quebec, the ship proceeded to Port Weller Drydocks.

There, on November 17, 1980, inspection revealed hull damage beyond economical repair. The vessel was thus refloated and cleared for Toronto arriving November 18.

Sold to Marine Salvage, the Lac Des Iles was stripped to the deck of cabins and equipment in April 1981. Resold for duty as a grain storage barge at Tampico, Mexico, the ship travelled south with Marlhill in tandem with the towing vessel Irving Birch.

Enroute they faced heavy weather. Lac Des Iles survived until June 1, and then plunged to the bottom of the Atlantic 62 miles ESE of Cape Charles, Virginia, in position 36.55 N, 74.44 W.

During 75 years of trading this ship was powered by an 1,800 horsepower triple expansion engine measuring 23-1/2 - 38 - 63 × 42. Two Scotch boilers 14'6" by 11'6" were originally coal fired but later burned oil. Her career as a steamer was far more successful than that of a barge.

LYMAN C. SMITH was once part of the "Typewriter" fleet (Great Lakes Graphics)

MARTHA HINDMAN is shown on July 3, 1971 (Pete Worden photo)

LAC DES ILES sailed two seasons for Q.&O. (Barry Andersen photo)

HELEN EVANS

By the time Helen Evans had joined the Q. & O. fleet she had already worked for three previous owners. Her service for the fourth would be but one year.

This vessel was built in 1906 for operation by the Jones and Laughlin Steel Corporation. She was constructed at Ecorse, Michigan, by the Great Lakes Engineering Works and, along with the first B.F. Jones, were the initial vessels in the J & L fleet.

The Laughlin measured 552 feet in overall length, 56 feet at the beam and 31 feet in depth. (168.3 × 17.1 × 9.5 metres). Tonnage was registered at 6,941 gross. An 1,800 horsepower triple expansion engine with cylinders of 23", 37", 63" and a 42" stroke provided power. Two Scotch boilers, 15 feet by 12 feet, produced steam until replaced by water tube models in 1950.

Millions of tons of iron ore moved from Lake Superior ports to the lower lakes aboard the James Laughlin. Much of it was delivered to Cleveland.

Wilson Marine Transit purchased the four remaining vessels in J & L's Interstate Steamship Company on November 15, 1952. The Wilson fleet was among the oldest on the lakes. It was founded in 1872 by Capt. Thomas Wilson and moved from sailing schooners to wooden steamers and then steel lakers. The first steel vessel on the Great Lakes, Spokane, was built for Wilson in 1886.

Wilson did not change the name of James Laughlin. They kept her busy carrying iron ore and coal. In addition, as was the custom in the 1950's, the ship occasionally hauled a deckload of automobiles. The vessel handled 62 vehicles per trip.

James Laughlin carried about 33 payloads a year with Superior, Wisconsin, the chief ore loading port and Cleveland the main discharge centre.

In the early sixties many ships were being retired by U.S. vessel operators. A number went for scrap while others joined Canadian registry to assist in the early transportation duties through the St. Lawrence Seaway.

Hindman Transportation acquired this vessel in the fall of 1964 and it operated the rest of the year in their colours under the old name.

When the 1965 season opened this ship had become the Helen Evans. As such it honored the daughter to Capt. George Hindman, the fleet's founder. Married to Parker Evans, who was then the General Manager of the firm, Mrs. Evans had for many years been active in the business affairs of the Hindman fleets.

JAMES LAUGHLIN underwent several changes before joining the fleet (Great Lakes Graphics)

Interestingly this was the third ship named for Mrs. Evans but the previous two vessels had carried her maiden name of Helen Hindman.

Helen Evans, the ship, worked in the Seaway trades. Tonnage was now registered at 7,534 gross, 5,150 net while she could carry 11,500 tons deadweight or 3.5,000 bushels of grain. To improve efficiency Hindman had the Helen Evans converted to burn oil for fuel in 1974 rather than coal.

Later, on September 21, 1977, steering problems caused the upbound ore laden ship to run aground on Whaleback Shoal near Brockville, on the St. Lawrence. It took two days to free the stuck laker.

Helen Evans joined Q. & O. for the 1978 season but the ship's age was beginning to show.

Yet the vessel managed to carry 19 cargoes that final year. Thirteen loads were of grain. These included corn out of Milwaukee and Saginaw, wheat from Chicago, Duluth and Thunder Bay, soybeans from Toledo and

Milwaukee plus a load of barley. Most of the grain was delivered to the St. Lawrence with discharge at Trois Rivieres, Port Cartier, Montreal and Quebec City.

Returning upbound Helen Evans carried five loads of ore from Port Cartier and Sept-Iles and one shipment of cement.

Helen Evans brought 337,500 bushels of soybeans from Milwaukee to Toronto as her final cargo arriving December 22. The next year the ship was sold to United Metals and towed to Hamilton.

Resold, Helen Evans was towed out of Hamilton August 30, 1980, by the tug Daniel McAllister. She then left Quebec City September 17 and arrived at Mamonal, Columbia, October 30, 1980, in a tandem tow with the Thornhill.

On July 14, 1981, work on scrapping Helen Evans was begun by S.I.T.S.A. at Cartagena, Columbia. Helen Evans, the proud old lakes veteran, was broken up.

HELEN EVANS operated one year in company colours and is shown retired at Hamilton in 1980 (AS)

PARKER EVANS / MARLHILL

The Parker Evans had an unusual background before joining the Q. & O. fleet. This bulk carrier had been involved in three major collisions and on each occasion the other ships sank and there were no casualties.

The first accident occurred in 1909 in the part of the St. Mary's River known as Mud Lake. The other ship was the first of four lakers named Henry Steinbrenner and it went down due to a 25 foot hole in her side. Fortunately the cabins remained above water so survival of crew was not a problem.

The featured vessel was almost new at the time having been built by the Great Lakes Engineering Works at Ecorse, Michigan, the previous year. Christened Harry A. Berwind, she sailed under Tomlinson's Mutual Steamship Company.

In 1917 the vessel passed to the Youngstown Steamship Co. and became Harvey H. Brown. This name was retained on joining the Interlake Steamship Co. in 1930.

During these early years the Berwind/Brown hauled regular shipments of ore, coal and occasional grain on the upper four Great Lakes. The arrival of the depresssion and the opening of the Welland Canal caused some changes in trading patterns and Harvey H. Brown came down the Welland Canal for the first time on October 4, 1932.

World War Two kept this ship busy carrying the raw materials for the steel making process and it was after that she had her second collision. This occurred in the fall of 1951 and sent the first George F. Rand to the bottom near Port Huron, Michigan. Again there were no casualties and the ship was salvaged.

Marine Salvage, the Port Colborne scrap firm purchased Harvey H. Brown in 1963 but they resold the vessel to Hindman Transportation the following year. The ship was registered in Canada as Parker Evans honouring the son-in-law of Capt. George Hindman.

This vessel was 552 feet long, 58 ft. at the beam and 32 feet in depth. (168.2 × 17.7 × 9.8 metres) Tonnage was registered at 7,815 gross, 5,735 net and she could carry 11,300 tons or about 380,000 bushels of grain.

Hindman used this ship throughout the Seaway and she was in their service June 5, 1977, when a collision occurred just below the Bluewater Bridge that links Canada and the United States at Port Huron and Sarnia. The upbound and coal-laden Sidney E. Smith Jr. was the other vessel and she sank on her side. Again no lives were lost but the ship was salvaged in two pieces and could only be used as a breakwall.

Parker Evans was repaired but shortly after returning to service had another misfortune colliding with the salt-water vessel Anna Katrin Fritzen on June 24 on a foggy Lake Huron. This time damage was minor.

Parker Evans joined Q. & O. in 1978 and ran one season. There were 18 cargoes that year with eight loads of corn, mostly from Milwaukee to Baie Comeau, six shipments of ore, two of wheat plus single loads of mixed grain and 5,727 tons of newsprint. The latter travelled from Baie Comeau to Chicago.

Her name became Marlhill in 1979 after a mining community near Belleville, Ontario from where Ontario Paper Company received a clay filler used in paper making.

HARVEY H. BROWN was also a former Interlake freighter (Emory Massman photo)

That year 22 payloads were handled and again corn dominated. In addition ore, wheat, malt, barley, coke, bauxite and mixed grains were carried. The vessel was laid up at Toronto December 12 with a storage load of 411,373 bushels of malt barley.

Marlhill began to fit-out for the 1980 season but boiler defects developed and the vessel remained idle at Toronto. She served briefly as a grain storage hull and then was sold for scrap. Then, this plan apparently fell through.

Instead, during April 1981, the hull was stripped to her deck. She cleared under tow on April 29 bound for Tampico, Mexico and a new career as a grain storage hull.

Unfortunately the vessel never arrived. On May 30, 1981, buffetted for days by strong winds, the Marlhill succumbed and broke loose of the tug Irving Birch and plunged to the bottom of the Atlantic. She went down 140 miles ESE of Cape Charles, Virginia, in heavy weather.

The vessel that had sent three others to the bottom could not escape a similar fate.

PARKER EVANS was another Hindman acquisition (AS)

The name MARLHILL sailed one year in the fleet (Barry Andersen photo)

THE CHARTERS

In addition to owned vessels, the company chartered ships for as short as one trip or as long as several years. Identifying all of the chartered craft is not the intent of this section.

Instead we will attempt to focus on some of the more significant, to these writers at least, charters.

Honoreva, chartered before being owned, qualifies as the first chartered vessel as well as the first owned outright.

With success at hauling pulpwood to Thorold established, company officials examined ways to deliver the end product, newsprint, via water. The first attempts were none too satisfying.

In 1914 and 1915 the vessels of the Rutland Steamship Company carried newsprint out of Thorold to Chicago as part of their freight cargo.

Then, in 1916, the Charles S. Neff was chartered for the task. But it could only carry half of what had been expected. As a result the ship's charter was discontinued.

Interestingly Charles S. Neff lasted into the 1960's and had five names and, at various times, French, Spanish and Brazilian owners.

Glenlyon was chartered in 1919 and although it carried a payload of 1,704 tons, loading and unloading was a slow and methodical procedure. Glenlyon lasted only a few more years before it stranded on Lake Superior November 1, 1924, and later broke up.

Railways handled much of the newsprint transportation but Col. McCormick did not give up on water transportation. Wahcondah was used for a time in the twenties and was more efficient as it had its own equipment for loading and unloading.

When the opening of the Fourth Welland Canal allowed larger freighters to Thorold some were used for winter storage and then shipped in the spring. The Cleveland-Cliffs bulk carrier Joliet, a vessel of 524 feet (159.7 metres) overall length, wintered at Thorold for 1931 - 32. When it cleared for the Tribune Dock at Chicago on April 24, 1932, it carried a Great Lakes cargo record for newsprint.

Water transportation through the Gulf of St. Lawrence was a risky venture during World War Two and ships were at a premium. Shutting down the Baie Comeau mill was a distinct possibility unless the newsprint could be distributed to the New York Daily News.

Arthur Schmon chartered three ships from the Federal Motorships Corporation. These were shallow draft vessels capable of operation on the Great Lakes and New York State Barge Canal to New York City. They were then used to carry newsprint south and returned with much needed bauxite for the Aluminum Company of Canada plant at Arvida, Quebec.

The three chartered vessels, Badger State, Buckeye State and Empire State were on bareboat charter until 1945.

Badger State was the reconstruciton of a former Canadian owned canal ship. It had been christened Fordonian in 1912 and later sailed as Yukondoc and Georgian. As the latter it opened Lock One of the Fourth Welland Canal on April 21, 1930, thus being the first upbound ship in the new waterway. Badger State was later lost on the Gulf of Mexico on January 14, 1946.

Buckeye State was a true barge canal vessel. It had been built at Ogdensburg, New York, in 1930 and lasted on the Great Lakes until heading south in 1956.

Empire State preceded Buckeye State at Ogdensburg and lasted until 1954. It arrived at Baltimore for scrap November 4, 1953, after running aground at Walton, Nova Scotia, the previous June.

Although the operation of these ships was expensive their service was essential to the success of the company during the war.

Numerous non-Q.&O. ships were used to bring pulpwood to Thorold. The biggest load of all came aboard the Geroge M. Carl.

This member of the Scott Misener Steamship Company fleet brought a record 4,699 cords from Baie Comeau to Thorold arriving July 24, 1972. The 617 foot (188.1 metre) laker was towed to Spain in 1984 and scrapped.

Chartered vessels were used to take newsprint to New York via the ocean route.

With production at Baie Comeau underway Louisiana was chartered from the American-Hawaiian Lines in 1938. It was a good start and as production increased a larger ship was needed.

The Norwegian flag Brand was chartered in 1939 for five years work but war intervened and the ship was not available in 1940.

The company-owned Colabee filled the gap until requisitioned in 1942 and then returned after the war.

Elin Hope, another Norwegian ship, was very useful in the early fifties. Later, on December 8, 1963, as Procyon, this ship was in collision on the St. Lawrence with Fort Albany. The latter, a small Canadian vessel, sank and five lives were lost.

Elin Hope also had a violent end. Sailing as Askok it arrived at Madras, India, May 8, 1967, on fire. It settled on the bottom, was pumped out, beached and scrapped.

Later long term charters to carry newsprint south from Baie Comeau were the 7,000 tons Norwegian freighter Baie Comeau and the West German Frank Schroder. The latter was ice strengthened and went as far south as Florida with newsprint for the Orlando Sentinel-Star.

Chartered tonnage made a valuable contribution to moving cargoes and contributed to the success of The Pulp and Paper Fleet.

ELIN HOPE made numerous trips to New York with newsprint (Morris Rosenfeld photo — Q.&O. files)

SOURCES OF INFORMATION

HISTORICAL JOURNALS:

Detroit Marine Historian — Marine Historical Society of Detroit.

Lake Log Chips — Institute for Great Lakes Research, Bowling Green State University.

Nor'Eastern — Lake Superior Marine Museum Association.

Scanner — Toronto Marine Historical Society.

Steamboat Bill — Steamship Historical Society of America.

Telescope — Great Lakes Maritime Institute.

TEXTS:

Trees to News, Carl Wiegman, 1953.

QNS — History of the Quebec North Shore Paper Company, Al Plosz, 1987.

Resume of Ontario Paper Company, Fred Byington, 1934.

Namesakes of the Lakes (series), John O. Greenwood, Freshwater Press.

The Lower St. Lawrence, Ivan S. Brookes, Freshwater Press, 1974.

Great Lakes Ships We Remember (Vol. I & II), Marine Historical Society of Detroit, 1979, 1984.

Greenwood and Dills Lakeboats (Annual), Freshwater Press.

Great Lakes Redbook (Annual), Fourth Seacoast Publishing Co.

Lloyds Register of Ships

NEWSPAPERS:

St. Catharines Standard
Port Huron Times Herald
Hamilton Spectator
Port Colborne News
Welland Evening Tribune

Watertown Daily Times
Goderich Signal Star
Toronto Globe and Mail
Thunder Bay Chronicle
  —Journal